"I'VE GOT TO TALK TO SOMEBODY, GOD reveals an honest baring of a woman's heart, simplicity of language, and immense reality. *This book is for every woman, every day.*"

—Catherine Marshall

DAILY BEAUTY

"Marjorie Holmes writes with a rare and unusual talent for releasing deep, inner feelings. Few people possess that ability. Her prayers will give much comfort to many people—especially those who have had similar deep concerns to which she addresses her prayers."

—Margaret Chase Smith, United States Senator, Maine

"In reading these beautiful prayers for everyday living—for every age—I can't think of a more wonderful practical gift than I'VE GOT TO TALK TO SOMEBODY, GOD—for my family —my friends—and certainly for me. A reference book of clear thinking for all occasions, for all times, but I am especially grateful that it has been published to read *now!*"

—Mary Martin

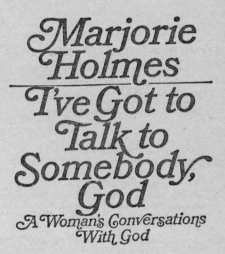

Marjorie Holmes
I've Got to Talk to Somebody, God
A Woman's Conversations With God

Illustrated by Betty Fraser

BANTAM BOOKS
NEW YORK · TORONTO · LONDON · SYDNEY · AUCKLAND

This edition contains the complete text
of the original hardcover edition.
NOT ONE WORD HAS BEEN OMITTED.

I'VE GOT TO TALK TO SOMEBODY, GOD
A WOMAN'S CONVERSATIONS WITH GOD

A Bantam Book / published by arrangement with
Doubleday

PRINTING HISTORY
Doubleday edition published February 1969
Doubleday Book Club alternate selection
Bantam edition published November 1971
35 printings through April 1988

Some prayers also appeared in WOMAN'S DAY, CHRISTIAN HERALD,
THIS WEEK, HOUSTON CHRONICLE, CATHOLIC DIGEST and in publi-
cations of the United Methodist Church.

Back cover photograph of the author by Vera Steele

ISBN 0-553-26428-1

Published simultaneously in the United States and Canada

PRINTED IN THE UNITED STATES OF AMERICA

KR   44 43 42 41 40 39 38 37 36

For Hope

Acknowledgment

The following prayers appeared originally in THE EVENING STAR, Washington, D.C., Copyright © 1966, 1967, 1968 by The Evening Star Newspaper Co.: "For a Friend" as "Prayer for a Friend;" "I'm So Worried About Money" as "Money Worries;" "Night Duty" as "Mother Answers Voice in Night;" "A Prayer for Peeling Potatoes" as "Potato—A Thing to be Grateful for;" "Bring Back the Children" as "A Mother's Arms Aren't Long Enough;" "Color" as "Bright Colors Bring Beauty;" "Order" as "Psalm for an Apron Pocket;" "On Making Beds" as "A Prayer for Making Beds;" "A Mother's Prayer in the Morning" as "Mother's Prayer at Morning."

Contents

Introduction

Descartes said, "Because I think, I am."
Because I am, I pray.

Prayer, to the thinking person, is almost inescapable. Even when, like Job, we cry out against God to challenge or deny him, we are praying. Call it nature, instinct, what you will, man is forever driven to try to make contact with the mysterious author of his own being.

We do this not to appease this force or to curry favor for some hoped for life beyond this one. We do this because *we've got to talk to somebody*. Especially in times of disappointment, trouble, despair.

The psalmist did this. Lying on some silent hillside after a bloody battle, or simply tending his flocks, he sang of his enemies and his agonies, his mistakes, his remorse, his shattered dreams; he pled desperately for solace and for aid. Sometimes he quarreled with God, often he rejoiced and exalted him. And again and again he spoke of his burning thirst to find and know his maker.

Today there are few such silent hillsides. We are crowded in upon one another. We are assaulted on all sides by radio, television, the printed word. We are taught to verbalize from a tender age. We have made almost a fetish of "communication."

Yet today there is so little genuine communication. The very push and pressure of living among so many people has driven us deeper inside ourselves. There, despite all the talk that swirls around us, we are locked in a lonely prison. It is a secret and special place, a place for our own protection, yet a place of anxieties and fears, where the loneliness can be intolerable, unless we find God there.

I grew up in a very healthy, vigorous, old-fashioned church where prayer was public and loud and frequently emotional, or something you rattled off in private to get it over with. Yet there was another kind of praying that stirred and nudged and worked within me even then. Whose voice would not be stilled even during the years of agnosticism and near atheism which many of us must undergo.

Eventually my own common sense rescued me from my so-called intellectualism. The patent falsity of an accidental universe (with its immutable laws, the incredible complexities of its many life forms, the marvel of the mind alone!) became self-evident. I began a sincere search for God and for spiritual enlightenment. During this period I read many books, some of them very helpful indeed.

I learned that simply to ask a blessing upon one's circumstances, whatever they are, is somehow to improve them, and to tap some mysterious source of energy and joy. I came upon one of the most ancient and universal truths—that to affirm and to claim God's help even before it is given, is to receive it. But whenever such books and writings attempted to set forth formulas, protocols of prayer by which one might better reach the ever-listening ear, they lost me. I became self-conscious, resistant, restless. No doubt they are very valuable to anyone with mystical inclinations, or who has or is willing to take the time. But for the average, busy, groping, faulty individual, there must be a more direct, attainable way.

Half guiltily, I realized that the only times I really felt in contact with what I sought, and drew help and encouragement from it, were those spontaneous times when prayers simply leaped up of their own volition, in words, in songs, sometimes even in such acts as dancing, swimming, or scrubbing a floor.

A sense of being able to talk to somebody, or of expressing adulation and gratefulness through ordinary, everyday acts. And a growing conviction that while it is good and right to go to a formal place of worship, it is even more important to worship God wherever we are. All altars are not confined to churches. Your altar may be your desk, the machine you operate, the kitchen stove. The Lord of Life may be known and adored through any deed that we dedicate to him and to the benefit of other people, whether that deed be typing a letter, turning out shoes, or making a family's dinner.

Christ walked the earth as a human being, administering to human needs. He spoke the tongue of his times, and surely in the most direct, unaffected way. It would be hard to improve upon his simple, forthright example.

The words which follow here are less prayers than a woman's conversations with God. Any woman's—for almost every woman has probably felt or expressed their essence many times. The ability to talk things over with God has cleared up confusion and led to a joyful new awareness, self-identification, and communion for me. My hope is that it will lead you to a renewed discovery of the tremendous release and comfort there is to be found in a living, loving, always listening God.

I've Got to Talk to Somebody, God

I've Got to Talk to Somebody, God

My heart hath talked of thee, Seek ye my face;
Thy face, Lord, will I seek.

PSALM 27:8

I've Got to Talk to Somebody, God

I've got to talk to somebody, God.

I'm worried, I'm unhappy. I feel inadequate so often, hopeless, defeated, afraid.

Or again I'm so filled with delight I want to run into the streets proclaiming, "Stop, world, listen! Hear this wonderful thing."

But nobody pauses to listen, out there or here —here in the very house where I live. Even those closest to me are so busy, so absorbed in their own concerns.

They nod and murmur and make an effort to share it, but they can't; I know they can't before I begin.

There are all these walls between us—husband and wife, parent and child, neighbor and neighbor, friend and friend.

Walls of self. Walls of silence. Even walls of words.

For even when we try to talk to each other new walls begin to rise. We camouflage, we hold back, we make ourselves sound better than we really are. Or we are shocked and hurt by what is revealed. Or we sit privately in judgment, criticizing even when we pretend to agree.

But with you, Lord, there are no walls.

You, who made me, know my deepest emotions, my most secret thoughts. You know the good of me and the bad of me, you already understand.

Why, then, do I turn to you?

Because as I talk to you my disappointments are eased, my joys are enhanced. I find solutions to my problems, or the strength to endure what I must.

From your perfect understanding I receive understanding for my own life's needs.

Thank you that I can always turn to you. I've got to talk to somebody, God.

I Don't Feel Loved Any More

Oh, Lord, I don't feel loved any more; I don't feel wanted.

My children are so thoughtless. They demand so much of me and take it without appreciation. They overlook the things they could do for me, and when I ask their help they cruelly rebel.

My husband is too preoccupied with problems even to suspect this awful vacancy I feel. I scarely know my neighbors; and my friends are too busy with their own concerns to really care.

Who would care, Lord, if I disappeared tomorrow? Who would really care? I know I am needed, and for that reason alone I would be missed. But *wanted*, Lord, really wanted as a person, for myself?

You, Lord, you alone know and love and care about me as a person. In you alone I find my understanding and my reassurance.

Help me now to draw upon that reassurance and take some of it back into all my relationships. As I seek that loving reassurance, I somehow know that other people do care deeply about me too, despite their seeming indifference. They would be shocked and hurt if they thought I doubted them.

Perhaps they don't think I see and care about them as people, either, but only as a responsibility or a comfort to myself. Thank you for this insight, Lord. Oh, give us all back reassurance. Let us all feel loved and wanted.

I'm So Worried About Money

Oh, God, give me more faith in your abundance.

Help me to stop worrying about money so much. Let me spend less time fretting about material things.

I often envy other people their possessions. Forgive me. I sometimes feel an actual pain in the presence of people whose dress and manner speak of ease and wealth. Forgive me this very real sin.

I do not covet—no, for I don't wish them less. Only I am anxious for more, so much more. And this is wrong.

It is putting emphasis upon the wrong things.
It bespeaks my lack of faith.

Lord, help me to remember how generously
you have endowed the earth.

That you have lavished upon us more food
than any of us can consume. More clothing than
any of us can wear. More treasures than we can
carry.

And that it is your will that each of us have
his portion. A fine full portion to meet all our
needs.

Help me to realize what my real needs are.
And to be thankful. For so long as I trust in you
all these needs are being, and will be met. . . .

(You said it is hard for a rich man to enter the
kingdom of heaven. Perhaps it's even harder for
a poor man who wants to be rich!)

I've Said "Yes" Once Too Often

Oh, God, I've done it again, I've said "Yes"
once too often and now I'm stuck with this extra
job.

How will I manage to accomplish everything?
All these committees, all these meetings, all these
phone calls.

Right now I don't see where there'll be enough time in the day (or night). I don't see where my strength is coming from.

Only you will help me. You will give me strength. You will give me the intelligence to manage. You, who created time, will even give me that.

Now let me quietly thank you for this challenge. If I'm a fool to take on so much—all right, you, who made me so, will not leave me stranded. You will fortify, you will supply my needs.

Bless the people with whom I'll be involved. Bless the job I've undertaken, and I know it will prove worthy of the efforts I bring to it.

I'm Showing My Age

> Behold, thou hast made my days as it were a span long, and mine age is even as nothing in respect of thee.
>
> PSALM 39:5

Oh, God, dear God, I'm showing my age.

I'm not young and beautiful any more, the way my heart imagines. When I look in the mirror I could cry. For I look just what I am—a woman growing older.

And I protest it, Lord. Perhaps foolishly, I am stricken.

"Vanity, vanity, all is vanity," the Bible says. But is vanity truly such a fault? You, who made women with this instinctive hunger to hang onto personal beauty, must surely understand.

Dear God, if this be vanity, let me use it to some good purpose.

Let it inspire me to keep my body strong and well and agile, the way you made it in the beginning. May it help me to stay as attractive as possible for as long as possible—out of concern for other people as well as myself. For you, who made women, also know that when we feel attractive we're a lot easier to live with.

But oh God, whatever happens to my face and body, keep me always supple in spirit, resilient to new ideas, beautiful in the things I say and do.

If I must "show my age" let it be in some deeper dimension of beauty that is ageless and eternal, and can only come from you.

Don't let me be so afraid of aging, God. Let me rejoice and reach out to be replenished; I know that each day I can be reborn into strength and beauty through you.

I Made a Mess of Things

Lord, I acted like a darned fool. I brought all this mess upon myself. Now bless me. Help me. Give me the courage to face up to my own mistakes.

Let my remorse be of some benefit. When I have plunged deeply enough into remorse maybe I'll be cleansed enough to face the facts about myself.

I was wrong. I erred. My reasons for erring are complicated and maybe justified—yet that is no help to anybody now. Least of all me.

Lord, I've already prayed for the other people harmed in all this and am doing what I can to make amends.

Now quite frankly, I'm praying for myself.

I acknowledge the blame. I am suffering the consequences. Please don't forsake me.

Help Me to See My Faults

Help me to see the truth about myself, however bitter that truth may be.

Help me to see my faults and not be over-powered by their number. Help me not to be discouraged by their gravity. (Keep me from a futile monologue of my mistakes. Let me remember, and be thankful, that I have virtues too!)

Lord, give me the sense to see my faults and the courage to attack them. Not all at once, but one by one, starting with my worst. Then, when I have that one pretty well under control, to proceed to the others.

Give me the will to do this, Lord. And the strength and the patience to keep on trying even when I fail.

Be tolerant of me in this struggle—and help me to be tolerant with myself.

Take These Hostilities

My heart is filled with hostilities this morning, Lord. Things have gone wrong in so many areas of my life. So many people, all at once, have disappointed me, dismayed me, hurt me, let me down.

Lord, help me not to compound this sense of shock and pain by blaming you too. Help me to remember that, prayers or no prayers, how people act is not your fault.

You are simply our creator, our confessor, our

help, and our only true hope. And we, your creations, are so faulty and out of step with what you would have us be and do.

Lord, erase these hostilities from me so that I may approach this day in peace. Lord, help me not to put my faith in people, but in you.

I'm Tired of All These Crises

How much are we supposed to stand, God? How much can the human spirit bear?

Trial is piled upon trial. And before one crisis is survived another bears down.

I am buffeted and bruised; I am knocked almost witless, yet I know I must keep my wits about me. I must keep my senses and remain strong, I must proceed.

It is as if these crises bear human faces and they encompass me like enemies, knocking me this way and that between them, crying for my help even as they beat me well nigh unconscious.

God, how much more can I stand?

Help me, Lord, help me to keep my sanity and my strength. God, please take some of these interminable problems from me. Disperse them, deal with them through some other channel. Surely I have been used enough. Surely I have been pursued and caught and used enough. There is not much left.

Lord, restore me. Give me strength.

But oh, release me for a little while too. Please give me a respite from these problems.

Tribulation

God, help me to remember that life is full of tribulation. And though you do not always deem it right or wise to help me, yet you *are* helping simply by being there.

My strength comes from you. Thank you.

My courage comes from you. Thank you.

Deep, deep within me, implanted by your very hands, is my determination, my toughness, my will to survive.

Though life batter and bruise me and try to tear me to pieces, it will not succeed. I will bare my teeth and smile into the face of life and thank you for it.

Like Job, I will not blame you. I will not curse you. I will not deny you. For you have created me to cry as well as to rejoice, above all, to endure.

You have not abandoned me. You have not left me comfortless.

One who suffered far more than I is with me always. And will be with me till the end.

The Tree

I will lift up my eyes and gaze into the face of the Lord for help.

He who has made the heavens and the earth and all the people on it has the power to help me. And I know that he will.

He who has made the tree in my backyard— this strong and mighty tree that lived long before I existed and will go on living, no doubt, long after I die—he has made me too.

Am I not as dear in his sight as that tree?

Isn't my fragile flesh as precious as its rough bark?

Aren't my arms which reach out to him in supplication as significant to him as the branching arms of that tree?

The wind sways the tree, but it holds fast.

It bows but it does not break—as I will hold fast and not be broken by the winds of life now.

The roots of the tree go deep, deep into the earth—as my heart's roots go deep into the life of my family.

He who made the earth itself and this single tree, he will not forsake me.

He is the source of survival. He is the source of all power. I claim his strength and his loving help.

He is as real and as close as the tree.

I Was So Cross to the Children

Yea, the sparrow hath found her an house, and
the swallow a nest, where she may lay her
young.

PSALM 84:3

I Was So Cross to the Children

Oh, God, I was so cross to the children today. Forgive me.

Oh, God, I was so discouraged, so tired, and so unreasonable. I took it out on them. Forgive me.

Forgive me my bad temper, my impatience, and most of all my yelling.

I cringe to think of it. My heart aches. I want to go down on my knees beside each little bed and wake them up and beg them to forgive me. Only I can't, it would only upset them more.

I've got to go on living with the memory of this day. My unjust tirades. The guilty fear in their eyes as they flew about trying to appease me. Thinking it all their fault—*my* troubles, my disappointments.

Dear God, the utter helplessness of children. Their vulnerability before this awful thing, adult power. And how forgiving they are, hugging me so fervently at bedtime, kissing me good night.

And all I can do now is to straighten a cover, move a toy fallen out of an upthrust hand, touch a small head burrowed into a pillow, and beg in my heart, "Forgive me."

Lord, in failing these little ones whom you've put into my keeping, I'm failing you. Please let your infinite patience and goodness fill me tomorrow. Stand by me, keep your hand on my shoulder. Don't let me be so cross to my children.

For a Wanted Child

Oh, God, thank you for the child I carry.

I am in love with it as I am in love with my husband and my life—and you.

I walk the world in wonder. I see it through new eyes.

All is changed, subtly but singingly different. The beauty of sunlight upon the grass, the feel of its warmth along my arms. It is cradling me in tenderness as I shall cradle this child one day.

I am mother and child in one, new as a child myself, innocent, excited, amused, surprised.

I marvel at my changing body. It is as sweet and new to me as when I was a little girl. Even its symptoms are less of misery or fatigue than signals of its secret. "See how important I am," my body claims. "Feel my insistence as I make and shape this child for you."

God, I am happy. God, I am sad. God, I am vital—alive, alive. Life has me in its hands. Life is moving me in an immutable direction that I don't want to resist and couldn't if I tried.

It is almost comical, this sweet and stern insistence. It is like night and day and the changing of the seasons. "Stop, stop!" I might as well cry to the winds or the sea.

No, no, I am in for it now, and I rejoice, though I am also a little bit afraid. The labor, the delivery, the care. But it is an exciting kind of anxiety. It is part of the privilege of being female.

Oh, God, bless this body in which the mystery of life is working. Let it be equal to its job.

And bless the tiny marvel it is responsible for. Your handiwork! Oh, bless my baby too—let it be whole and beautiful and strong.

For a Child Who's Struggling at School

Dear Lord, please bless this child and give him understanding.

Break down the barriers that are keeping him from grasping these skills, this knowledge. Stir and awaken his now dreaming mind.

Bless his books. Let your power and love work through them to excite and delight him so that their message is clear and strong.

Bless his tools—his paper and pencils and crayons, so that they become lovely and sure, a source of joy to his hands.

Bless his teacher. Give her patience. Give her understanding. Give her the ability to guide him out of dark confusion into the light of comprehension and command.

Bless us, his mother and father. Help us to help him by being smarter ourselves. Halt our sometimes scolding tongues. Check our worry and concern. Fill us with so much pride in him— and so much faith in you—that he will feel it as a mighty force that encourages and moves him on.

For in you is all wisdom. And that wisdom is a part of our child.

For an Unexpected Child

Dear God, it's true, we're going to have another child. And I am aghast, I am stunned. I didn't expect this, I didn't want it, and there's no use pretending—to you or to myself—I don't want it now.

With so many childless women longing for babies, why have you chosen me? You, who are the Author and Giver of Life, as the prayer book says—why not one of them? Why me, why me?

I don't need or want this gift. I am not grateful for it. I don't understand your ways.

"Some day it will be a great comfort to you," the doctor says. And some deep abiding instinct assures me he is right. But that is small comfort *now*.

Then there is that other cliché, "The Lord will provide." And you will, financially you will, you always have.

Yet I don't want to have to wait for that proof either. Provide for me *now*. Provide for this child. Provide me with love and joy and a feeling of welcome for this little new unexpected life.

Thank you, God, for the quiet, peaceful, stimulating visit you let me have with these dear friends, the childless couple.

Thank you for the memory of their beautiful home where nothing is broken or worn or fingermarked. I am grateful for the good conversation we shared over a good dinner, with good music in the background instead of clamoring voices and spilled milk.

I rejoice for them in their freedom—to go to concerts and parties, to travel, or just be alone with each other. They're sorry they never had a family, they tell me. They sometimes grieve for the children they never had. Yet anyone can see that they're not lonesome—they have so many friends. And that, without children to worry and fight about, they may be closer than some of us who have.

Thank you that this has been given them to compensate. Thank you for their happiness, for happiness is rare.

And now, Lord, please rid me of this awful discontent. This feeling that there ought to be something wrong with the picture, and a curious sense of injustice that there isn't.

Cleanse me of this emotion that borders on envy. Sweep it from me in a tide of blessing.

Continue to shine upon my friends' home and

their health and their future, and their great kindness to me.

And bless my children. Bless the fact of their creation—that I could conceive them and bring them into this world, in spite of all the problems they involve, all the sacrifice.

Thank you for the vast wealth of experience they have given me. I am not richer than my friends—no, but not poorer either. For I am rich in a different way:

Thank you for the noisy music of my children's voices, for the living, laughing, jewel-brightness of their eyes. Thank you that no mink coat could ever warm me the way I am warmed when I hold even one of them tight in my arms.

Bless even this battle-scarred house. Thank you that I see it now for what you must have meant it to be: A mansion. The mansion of my own dumb, glorious, amazing, rich fertility!

A Mother's Prayer in the Morning

Thank you, Lord, for this glorious day.

Bless the carpet beneath my feet and the bombardment of hot and cold water that freshens my waking skin.

Bless the breakfast I am cooking for my family, and the special music of morning around me—doors banging, the clatter of forks and plates, the rattle of lunch boxes, children demanding "Mother!"

Thank you for my healthy available presence that is able to cope with them.

Bless the husband who provides all this. Be with him as he sets off for work; fill him with a sense of his own worth and achievement, enrich and enliven his day.

Bless the school buses and their drivers, let them transport our children safely.

Bless the teachers and that marvelous institution that claims my offspring for the next important hours. Please let them be good there, happy there, bright and able to grasp the lessons there, and oh, thank you that they're well enough to *be* there.

Now bless this quiet house—even its confusion and disorder which speaks so vividly of its quality of life. Thank you that I have the time and the strength to straighten it.

And thank you for the freedom to sit down with a cup of coffee before I begin!

Night Duty

Oh, Lord, I hear it again, that little voice in the night, crying, "Mommy!"

At least I think I hear it. It may be my imagination. It may be just the wind. Or if not, maybe it will stop in a minute, the child will go back to sleep. . . .

(Oh, let it be just the wind. Or let him go back to sleep. I'm so tired. I've been up so many nights lately. I've got to get some sleep too.)

But if it's true, if it's one of them needing me and it isn't going to stop, if I must go—help me.

Lift me up, steady me on my feet. And make me equal to my duty.

If he's scared give me patience and compassion to drive the fears of night away.

If he's ill give me wisdom. Make me alert. Let me know what to do.

If he's wet the bed again, give me even more patience and wisdom and understanding (and let me find some clean sheets).

Thank you, Lord, for helping my weary footsteps down this hall.

Thank you for sustaining me too as I comfort and care for the child.

Thank you for my own sweet . . . sweet . . . eventual sleep.

Respite

Oh, Lord, thank you for this little space between crises in our family. Thank you for this probably brief span of peace.

Right now nobody is ill. Thank you. Right now nobody is in trouble. Thank you. Right now I am coasting, resting. It is as if I am walking across a pleasant meadow with only the happy chiming of birds in my ears and the sunlight as of some wondrous love upon my face.

The familiar cries of sorrow, distress, imploring pleas, and arguments are still. Thank you. The familiar burdens seem to be lifted, the problems for the moment all resolved. I rejoice in this sense of lightness and release.

It is common sense that tells me that this lovely respite cannot last, and not really my lack of faith.

For now, let me simply be thankful for this respite. Let me be revitalized by it. Let me draw from it physical strength and spiritual resources for the inevitable crises and conflicts to come.

Thank you, God, for this precious span of peace.

Put My House in Order

In thee, O Lord, have I put my trust; let me
never be put to confusion.

PSALM 31:1

Order

I will trust the Lord to bring order into my life and into my house.

In his presence there can be no real chaos and confusion and dirt for he is peace and purity and order—and he is here.

He lives within these walls as he lives within my heart.

He sometimes stops me as I fret and struggle and scold, and says, "Don't be discouraged." He reminds me that we are all his untidy children, but he loves us all—even as I love these who cause me so much work.

As I move from room to room picking up other people's possessions, he reminds me how abundant is life that it strews in my family's path so many good things.

He bids me look out of the window and see the abundance of the fields, the woods, the water.

The very earth is strewn with the bright ownings and discards of its living things: sticks and branches and leaves, shells, snakeskins, nests and weeds, and feathers and flowers.

The very water carries these things on its breast. The wind blows them about.

Yet Mother Nature does not despair—no matter how many times she must do it all over.

He reminds me that back of everything, governing all, is order. Absolute order.

I will trust the Lord to bring that order into my house.

On Making Beds

Dear Lord (or maybe his mother), please help me to learn the simple secrets of making a bed. However I try, there are always these bumps and wrinkles, or something's trailing, and the pillows never quite match. But even if I never do learn, let me be conscious of how lucky I am to have these comfortable beds.

Thank you that my children aren't sleeping on ragged quilts on a floor, or on straw in a mud hut. Or huddling like animals on city streets, as hordes of people still do.

God, surely all mankind is equally dear to you. I don't know why millions of your children are doomed to live in want, while the rest of us have it so good. I know that you don't will it so, yet your world is bitterly unfair.

Have pity on them, Lord. Bless all your creatures. Wherever a man, woman or child, or even an animal lies down tonight, let him be warm, let him be comfortable. Bless his rest.

Meanwhile, forgive my foolish fussing as I struggle with this bed.

Thank you for the good mattress, the crisp white sheets, the nubby blankets, the lovely spread. Thank you that I am physically able to see them, feel them, and despite a few bumps and wrinkles, cope with them.

Thank you for the task and the trial and the privilege of making beds.

A Prayer for Peeling Potatoes

I don't peel potatoes as often as my mother did, Lord, but when I do, I'm grateful. I suddenly feel near to you, my creator. And near to the past which produced me, near to all the people from which I came.

For hungry though we often were for other things, Lord, you always supplied us bountifully with potatoes. And we never got tired of them —baked, boiled, fried, or eaten raw with salt. (We even made potato sandwiches sometimes, after school.)

What a variety of possibilities you put into this homely food. What beauty you thought to include, what pleasure. . . . The vines with their starry blossoms. And digging for them—as we have to dig for many of life's best things—to find them clinging like small brown gnomes to the parent root, or scattered about like treasures.

Potatoes. Dusty, earth-colored potatoes. Humble, plain, yet holding within their white flesh the stuff of life for our survival. The miracle of nourishment.

A potato. To feel its weight like a nugget in my hand. To prepare it for its place in my family's meal. This is to see and know absolute beauty for a minute; this is to participate in the very essence of your plan.

For as I cook this potato I too am performing the simple, necessary function you meant for me. I too am creator.

The Dishes

Oh, God, I sometimes think I can't face these dishes one more time. Not even one more time.

You know I don't mind the cooking; cooking is creative. I have a happy consciousness of your presence when trying to decide what to serve for dinner, mixing and fixing things.

But, like the children (forgive me!), you don't seem to be around very much when it comes to the cleaning up.

This clutter of pans—less than an hour ago bubbling and steaming with things that gave off a delicious smell of promise; now nothing but empty enemies demanding, "Scrape me, scour me, put me away."

And the foods on which I lavished such loving effort—all vanished, except for dismal scraps, the mess on forks and plates.

It's as if there's a witch, unbidden to the banquet but always hovering in a corner, ready to triumph, wreak her ruin in the end.

Only she won't. I won't let her, even if *I* have to be the witch, demanding, "Come on now, help. Whose turn is it to do the dishes?"

Because the help I really want is their companionship, Lord. Cohorts in this inescapable assault. Their voices even in argument, their voices in discussion and laughter above the rattle of silver and the clatter of the pans.

When they join me, the water runs scalding hot, the suds leap high, and so do my spirits again. And I feel that you join us too through the confidences we share, the eager dreams. Soon, almost too soon, the dishes are finished, the kitchen once more orderly and clean.

Thank you, Lord, that out of frustration and confusion can come this sense of fulfillment and content. Help me to remember it the next time I think I just can't face the dishes alone again.

I need you then too.

Prayer for Ironing

Dear God, as I iron these clothes for my family, please make me aware not what a chore it is, but what a blessing:

That we have so many clothes to keep them warm. So many clothes to make them happy—pretty dresses, bright plaid shirts. Let me be thankful even for the trousers, hard as they are to press. Let me be thankful for having sons.

Thank you for this iron, with its simple yet marvelous power—heat and steam. Thank you for this sturdy ironing board. Thank you for spray starch, which has cut down my dampening time and makes everything so sweetly crisp. Thank you for this tumbled treasury of garments and tablecloths and pillow slips.

Thank you for the strength to make them smooth. And for all the hours of my life that I have been able to do this job, however I have dreaded it or put it off.

Give me the patience, please, to teach my own daughters this ancient art that every woman should know. And to teach my sons, as well, so that they, if they ever have to, can do their own.

And dear Lord, give me a spiritual strength to match this strength I bring to the smoothing of these clothes. As you have equipped my hands to guide this iron, please equip me with the wisdom to guide my children, to smooth out the wrinkles in their lives as well.

Scrubbing a Floor

Thank you for the privilege of scrubbing this floor.

Thank you for the health and the strength to do it. That my back is straight and my hands are whole.

I can push the mop. I can feel the hard surface under my knees when I kneel.

I can grasp the brush and let my energy flow down into it as I erase the dirt and make this floor bright and clean.

If I were blind I couldn't see the soil or the patterns of the tile or the slippery circles shining.

If I were deaf I couldn't hear the homely cheerful sounds of suds in the bucket, the crisp little whisper of brush or mop.

I would miss the music of doors banging and children shouting and the steps of people coming to walk across this bright expanse of floor.

Lord, thank you for everything that has to do with scrubbing this floor.

Bless the soap and the bucket and the brush and the hands that do it. Bless the feet that are running in right now to track it. This I accept, and thank you for.

Those feet are the reason I do it. They are the living reasons for my kneeling here—half to do a job, half in prayer.

A floor is a foundation. A family is a foundation. You are our foundation.

Bless us all, and our newly scrubbed floor.

Color

Oh, God, how grateful we all should be for color.

For blue skies and blue eyes and this little blue dress that I'm hanging on the line.

For oranges vivid in the brown basket that sits upon my kitchen table. For the purple grapes that choke the fence, and the lavender cups of morning glories against a white garage.

What a lovely thing—the interplay of colors in a paisley blouse. A throw rug. A bracelet. A vase on the shelf. I think of all the unsung artists and craftsmen who have produced them, and the marvelous routes and ways of trade and commerce that must weave and interplay—like the intermingling colors—to bring them all into my home to enrich and heighten the pattern of all our lives.

I am grateful, God, for all red things. For cannas, and scarlet cardinals. For the ruby red of cherries. The red on a woodpecker's throat. The bright living red of my own blood flowing. And the faded red of old boxcars or windbeaten barns.

I offer up thanks, dear God, for green. That leaves are green of countless shades—and so are the grasses and growths with which you've chosen to carpet your world. And that we, your people, are given gifts that enable us to copy those limitless greens in paint and fabrics, in wallpapers and leathers and dyes.

I am happy, Lord, for yellow. The golden yellow of sunshine, and butter, and daffodils, and autumn trees. For the lovely yellow—so rich, so intense—in an egg yolk, a lemon, a length of ribbon, a pair of bright new shoes.

And you gather up all these many colors into an arch of misty ribbons and turn them into a rainbow for our delight. As if the whole beautiful earth were being packaged up and tied with a bow.

How grateful we should be that you didn't give us a drab, sere world, or one in mere black and white. That you decided to make even people in so many shades of skin and hair and eyes. How dull it would be, Lord, if all races and all faces looked alike.

Thank you, God, for color. All the exciting hues that drench the earth and stir the senses. And for giving us the eyes with which to see them. Thank you, God, for the miracle of sight.

Unexpected Company

They'll be here soon, the company I wasn't expecting and really don't want very much— but thank you for them.

Bless this house (and help me to get it cleaned up in time). This kitchen (and help me to find in it something worthy of guests).

Bless my dear foolish husband who invited them, and me as I strive to be a good hostess and a good wife to him.

Bless this table that I'm preparing; these linens (thank you that they're clean); this china and silver, these candles, wobbly though they are. This room, this meal—may it all turn out to be shining and good and lovely, to compensate for my sense of distress, ill humor, of not wanting to bother.

Oh, Lord, thank you for these guests as they drive toward us (and make them drive slowly, please).

I send out thoughts of love toward them, I send out welcome, and these thoughts ease my nervousness and make me genuinely glad inside.

Thank you for their friendship. Thank you that they have called us and can come. Thank you for the greetings and the news and the ideas that we will exchange.

Fill us all with rejoicing. Make us feel your presence among us. Bless our coming together in the warm hospitality of my house.

Oh, God, how I dread cleaning the refrigerator. And I mean that not as an oath, but a prayer.

There it stands, singing away so faithfully, keeping our foods fresh for us. Reluctantly I open it, and instead of being grateful for its overflowing plenty, I want to back away and slam the door.

Instead, let me pause a moment and thank you. How generously you provide for us. We are never hungry. There is more than enough to go around—there are even leftovers.

Leftovers. A nuisance, yes, but also a symbol of your bounty. Quite literally our cups "runneth over."

And these cups, Lord. These chill bright bowls. Thank you for them and for all the foods they hold. What an infinite variety of things are here to please and nourish us. The eggs, so delicate and white in my hands. The milk, rich and heavy in its cartons. The bins of vegetables and fruit. The tangy globes of oranges, the moist green lettuce, the red meats, and yellow cheeses.

Everything that we need to survive you quietly put upon this earth for us, and the proof is here before me. Here on these crowded shelves.

Lord, forgive me for even a moment of irritation. Flood me with thankfulness.

Bless these shelves that I scrub and restore to order. Bless my hands as I work. And bless this task; make it no longer a source of dread, but a humble form of woman's worship—cleaning the refrigerator.

A Psalm for Going to Market

I will rejoice in the Lord as I set off to market with my children. I will give thanks unto the Lord for this good bright day.

I will praise him for this car at my disposal, the miracle of its body and its wheels and its engine and my ability to drive it. For I am but one of a horde of women who propel ourselves about the earth on errands and duties and jaunts of pleasure, in a manner that would be envied by the richest of charioted kings.

I will lift up my eyes to the beauty of the roadside in the morning, to the parks and playgrounds, to the schools and stores, to the houses large and small, all so marvelously equipped with devices and comforts for living.

I will open my eyes to the beauty of traffic lights, their glowing Christmas tree colors of scarlet and green. I will see the loveliness of the sunlit parking lot, and of mothers hastening to market, alone or with children trailing.

I will give thanks for the privilege of pushing a cart along the aisles, one child in the basket and another hitching rides. I will try not to lose patience, try not to scold. I will be grateful for the friends who pause to chat, and for the people who smile upon our little caravan.

I will rejoice and give thanks for the spaciousness and bounty of this place. For all the fragrant, gaily colored foods and products for my home. I will ask for the judgment to choose wisely.

I will rejoice and give thanks to my God who has provided the beauty and abundance of this my land, and this my neighborhood, and this my hour of marketing.

Whether my purse be large or small I will lift my eyes and my heart in humble gratefulness and worship him.

In Family Confusion

Oh, Lord, I've so much to do and the day seems to be flying in all directions.

There are errands to run, and the car won't start, and the only man who can fix it won't be in, they tell me, for another hour.

Clothes that were due haven't come from the cleaner's and I can't go after them and my husband *has* to have his suit for a trip right after lunch.

The house is a mess. The washer has broken down. The dog has just thrown up on the kitchen floor. Picking up some papers, I find our child has failed his last three history tests.

But now in the midst of all this confusion let me pause and think of you.

Let your peace and order and patience fill me.

Let me remember the ultimate harmony and pattern of the universe. How dependably the seasons and days run their courses, despite storms and catastrophes there too.

Let me remember your timelessness; you are eternal, there is truly time for everything that is truly important with you.

Thank you for this consciousness. For the re-assurance it gives me. Let it steady me in my panic, let me hold fast to it as I proceed, as calmly and as best I can, to cope with these things.

The Shining House

Oh, Lord, it's so lovely right now, this minute, my house that I've just cleaned up. Thank you. Bless it.

Everything is all shining, shining. The pans in the kitchen, the silver in the drawer, the bathroom bowls. I've turned on a few lamps and they bloom like shining flowers in the little garden of my house.

All of it is tidy, warm and shining, with the fire leaping, and even the bricks mirroring its dance because I've waxed them. Bless the fire, its cheery crackle, its warmth, its liveliness.

And bless me too as I stand full of love and sweet resolutions about keeping my house always so. Let me hold fast to the lovely image of order that will give way, all too soon, to the crumbs and trackings and chaos of living.

Bless and fortify me against the times when there won't be flowers on the mantel or a fire on the grate, or shining silver and bathroom bowls. Let me store up moments like this, right now, to cancel out the crossness and impatience with such inevitable hours.

Thank you, Lord, and keep guiding me back to them—these moments of perfection in my cleanly shining house.

The Tender Trap

Many waters cannot quench love, neither can the floods drown it.

SONG OF SOLOMON 8:7

Oh, Lord, I'm so tired and lonely and blue I'm a little afraid. I'm so sick of housework, sick of the children. They get on my nerves so I could scream (and do). I'm even sick of my husband right now—I wish he'd go away on a trip.

Or I wish *I* could get away for a change. My husband says okay, go; go visit my sister. But that's not it. Even if I managed to leave the children I'd be around hers. . . . No, I want something else that has nothing to do with women and children. I want to be somebody else for a while. Maybe the girl I used to be, or maybe a woman I haven't even met yet. A beautiful, poised woman with a mind and life of her own.

Only I can't. There's never any going back to what you used to be. And right now there is no going ahead. There is only the present which sometimes seems such a trap. As the play called it—*The Tender Trap*. Only it was funny in the play, and it was the man who felt trapped.

Maybe my husband feels trapped too, going day after day to the same job. Maybe the people he has to deal with get on his nerves too (only a man can't scream). . . . And the women who leave their houses and fight traffic or crowded buses to get to work every day. Maybe they're screaming, too, somewhere inside.

Lord, help me to realize how lucky I am here, right now, within this tender trap. Turn my fantasies of escape to some purpose. If there's a woman I haven't met yet, locked somewhere inside me, let her out.

Bless that person you surely meant me to be, instead of this self-pitying drudge. Recreate me in her image. Help me to see that she is not some superior creature that would evolve out of other circumstances, but that she lives inside me.

Lord, I now affirm and claim her. I claim her poise, her calm, her patience, her cheerfulness, her self-control. I claim her beauty. I claim her awakened mind.

I claim her for my children. She will be a better mother.

I claim her for my husband. She will be a better wife.

I claim her for all women who are feeling the confines of their tender traps. Bless them and help each of them to find her too.

The Hour of Love

Oh, God, thank you for this beautiful hour of love.

My dear is asleep now, but I am too filled with the wonder and joy of it to sleep just yet.

I stand at the window gazing up at your starriddled sky. I lean on the sill and gaze down upon your quiet earth.

How rich and fruitful it smells, how fragrant with life and the promise of life.

I see your trees reaching out as if to each other. For even trees must have mates to mature. Then they cast down their seeds and the rich fertile earth receives them to bear afresh.

I see the fireflies winking, hear the crickets and the locusts and the frogs. All are calling, calling, insistently, almost comically, "Here I am! Come. Come to me!"

"Male and female created he them," I think. For everything must have its opposite and meet with its opposite to be fulfilled.

Thank you, God, for this remarkable plan. Thank you for the hours of love it means.

I am as happy as one of the those crickets singing in the grass.

I feel as tall and strong and lovely as one of those outreaching trees. I feel as complete yet filled with promise as the earth teeming with its seeds.

Thank you, God, for making me a woman.

Money and Marriage

Dear God, surely it's not the love of money that is the root of all evil, at least in marriage—it is in not knowing how to divide it wisely. How much am I free to spend without feeling guilty? How much is my husband, without my resenting it? When I earn money is it mine to do with what I want? Or am I obliged to turn it over to him and then ask for some of it back?

I am all confused about this, Lord, I am upset. And my husband is too. But when we try to talk it over and come to some conclusions, either we hurt each other by being too frank, or we hold back and harbor the hurt of things left unsaid.

And there is too much worry about money in our marriage, Lord. The needs of a home and family never shrink and they never stop; they only multiply and swell.

They are crowding out fun and affection, they cast their shadow over our whole relationship. It is as if we were separated by a vast pile of paper—bills and mortgages and tax forms; or as if we were cut off from each other by a wall of material demands—the car, the house, the things the children need.

Dear Lord, restore to us some perspective. Guide us back to the essentials. Help us to realize that companionship is more important than even physical comforts; that material security means nothing if there isn't emotional security as well.

Dear God, please help us to resolve our misunderstandings. Give us either more money or more sense.

The Other Woman

I am all conf...
And my husband is too. But when we try to talk
is over and come to some conclusions. When we

This woman is attracted to my husband, Lord, and I don't know whether to be proud, amused, alarmed—or mad.

She plays up to him, she draws him out, she flirts with him. And in her presence he's a new man—more appealing, more witty, smarter, in a fine glow. And more gallant; he pays her little attentions he's long since stopped paying me.

I am annoyed, Lord, I'm upset—and ashamed of feeling so. Jealousy stings me, a shocked pang that, actually, I rather enjoy. It makes me want to play the martyr, retreating to lick my wounds. And it makes me want to punish him.

Oh, Lord, deliver me from these dangerous emotions. Help me to sort them out and not yield to the temptation to make things worse.

Help me to learn from them: That I do care very much about him and wouldn't want to lose him. But that maybe I haven't been showing it enough. Oh, Lord, help me to show it now, in the right ways.

And help me to learn, too, from this other woman. New ways to make my husband feel happy and attractive and important as a man.

The Coffee Klatch

Oh, God, I'm ashamed of women right now. And ashamed of myself.

I have just come from a coffee where all we did was berate our husbands. And the sweet taste of our pain was appalling. We loved it. For the moment we loved it more than pride or loyalty or self-respect; we loved it more than our men.

Dear God, there we were—women who claim men's protection and men's support. Women who want and need men. Yet taking apart the men we chose and promised before you to honor, exposing their faults to others.

No voice was raised in their defense. None of us mentioned their virtues, or acknowledged how much we depend on them. On this, like the rest, I was shamefully silent.

And now I cringe with self-contempt. How can I face my husband when he comes cheerfully home, tired from a hard day working for me?

Oh, Lord, don't let him see the misery in my eyes; don't let him sense my self-disdain. And let me make up to him for this foolish betrayal.

God, in the future guard me against temptation. Let your love and my love join forces to prevent me from taking part in this unfair female chorus.

The Quarrel

God, we quarreled again last night, and today my heart is sore. My heart is heavy. It is literally heavy, as if a leaden weight were hanging in my breast.

And part of its weight is that he is bowed with it too. I keep seeing him, his head low, his shoulders actually bowed under it as he trudged off to work.

I can hardly bear the image. I could hardly bear it then. I wanted to run out and stop him, say nothing is worth this awful estrangement, say I'm sorry. But I didn't. I let him go, afraid more words might only lead to more quarreling.

I turned my sore heart back into this house, so heavily haunted by the quarrel. I drag myself about my tasks here, trying to forget the things we said.

But the words keep battering away at my sore heart and aching head. However I try to turn them off, they repeat themselves incessantly, a kind of idiot re-enactment of a play so awful that you keep trying to run out of the theater. Only all the exits are locked. The play goes on and on—and the worst of it is I keep adding more lines to it, trying to improve my part in it, adding things I wish I'd said.

God of love, please let this play end! Open the exits of my mind. Let the blessed daylight of forgiveness and forgetting pour in.

Bless him wherever he is. Lift the weight of

this quarrel from his heart, his shoulders. I claim peace for him now, this minute. I claim and confirm your peace and joy for both of us when he returns.

When a Husband Loses Interest

My husband has lost interest in me, Lord. I feel it. I know it.

I am less to him than his easy chair. Less to him than his dinner. Less than the TV set or his friends or his hobby or his newspaper.

At least such things comfort him or give him enjoyment. But me—it is as if I am invisible to him. He does not see me. He scarcely ever touches me. Even at night he has no need of me; he is asleep before I get to bed.

Lord, where have I failed that he takes me so for granted? Is his blindness and indifference perhaps a reflection of my own blindness and indifference to myself?

If I am no longer physically attractive, let me improve. Give me the time, energy, imagination, yes and the money, to become more appealing.

If I have become dull and boring, wake me, shake me, let me read more, think more, do more to be a better companion.

If I have nagged or scolded or complained without realizing it, show me these faults clearly, help me to change.

Dear Lord, please awaken my husband to my presence once again. Make him see me, touch me, know me, love me as a woman once more. With your help I can become someone more worth seeing, touching, knowing, loving.

Thank you for revealing this better self.

To Live Without Sex

If I must live without sex, Lord, help me to do so gracefully. Don't let me become bitter and resentful, blaming you, the world, or anybody else.

Instead of self-pity, give me the strength and the cheerful acceptance that comes from self-respect.

Above all, give me understanding; the wisdom to sort out the complexities of this common human condition. It's so easy to confuse what the body thinks it needs and wants with what the mind and the world dictate. Protect me from this confusion, Lord, don't let me be misled.

Help me to remember, Lord, that many people endure afflictions and deprivations far worse. And that a great many people live happy, purposeful, inspiring lives that are devoid of sex.

Give me their secrets of acceptance, give me their grace.

If I am to live without sex, Lord, allow me to express and use this great force you have given me for some significant end.

Bring Joy Back into Marriage

I will trust in the Lord to bring joy back into my marriage.

I am so lonely. My husband is so lonely. We can't talk to each other any more. There is so little touching between us. We can't reach each other.

We pass like ships on a dark night at sea, fearful of drawing too close lest we crash. There is a great fog between us. We call out to each other, but the fog of our different interests and many concerns blurs the message.

The sound is harsh and forlorn. It is meaningless.

Even the occasions when we try to come together as man and wife are meaningless. It is worse than if we were strangers; strangers would take some interest in each other. But though we are supposed to love each other, and do, there is no interest, no delight.

Lord, let the light of your presence bring joy back into our marriage. Burn bright within each of us, to warm us and cheer us so that it breaks down the fog between us.

Dear Lord, shine through me as a person to reach my husband and draw close to him in love and joy, the way you meant us to.

The Good Days of Marriage

Dear Lord, thank you for the good days of marriage. The days when we wake up pleased with each other, our jobs, our children, our home, and ourselves.

Thank you for our communication—the times when we can really talk to each other; and the times when we understand each other without so much as a gesture or a word.

Thank you for our companionship—the times when we can work together at projects we both enjoy. Or work in our separate fields and yet have that sense of sharing that can only come when two persons' lives have merged in so many other ways so long. Thank you that we don't feel cut off from each other, no matter how divergent the things we do.

Thank you for our times of privacy. Our times of freedom. Our relaxed sense of personal trust. Thank you that we don't have to clutch and stifle each other, that we have learned to respect ourselves enough to respect the other's individuality.

Thank you, Lord, that despite the many storms of marriage we have reached these particular shores. Help us to remember them. Help us to hold fast to them, Lord.

A Psalm for Marriage

I am married, I am married, and my heart is glad.

I will give thanks unto the Lord for the love and protection of my husband. I will give thanks for the blessed protection and satisfaction of my home. I will give thanks that I have someone of my own to help and comfort and even to worry about, someone to encourage and to love.

My husband is beside me wherever I need to go. My husband is behind me supporting me in whatever I need to do. I need not face the world alone. I need not face my family alone.

I need face only myself and my God alone. And this is good. This is very good.

Whatever our differences, whatever our trials, I will give thanks unto the Lord for my husband and my marriage. For so long as I have both my husband and my God I am a woman complete, I am not alone.

Keep Me at It

Delight thou in the Lord, and he shall give thee
thy heart's desire. Commit thy way unto the
Lord and put thy trust in him, and he shall
bring it to pass.

PSALM 37:4–5

Keep Me at It

Keep Me at It

God, give me due respect for the abilities you have given me.

Don't let me sell them short. Don't let me cheapen them. Don't let me bury my talents through indecision, cowardice, or laziness.

Plant in me the necessary determination. Keep me at it.

Rouse in me the fires of dedication. Keep me at it.

Give me the energy, strength, and will power to bring your gifts to their proper fruition. Keep me at it.

When I falter or fall lift me up and set me back on my destined path. Keep me at it.

Oh, God, when the way seems dark and there is no light there, plant at least one small signal fire at the end of the long black tunnel that I may keep plodding steadily forward toward it.

When friends laugh at me, keep me at it.

When people tempt me away from it, keep me at it.

When others scorn what I have produced, let me not be discouraged. Keep me at it.

When those who have tried and failed or who have never tried at all, those who are envious or indolent, when such people would hurt me by spiteful words or acts, let me not be bothered. Return me to my task. Keep me at it.

Let nothing really matter but these precious

gifts you have entrusted to me. For their sake let me be willing and proud to make the sacrifice. Keep me at it.

Anger

Dear Lord, I'm angry—so angry.

Anger is consuming me like a raging fire.

I want to do something drastic. I want to scream.

Don't let me. Control me. Bless me, help me.

Bless and steer this anger into something constructive instead of tearing me up like this. Help me to channel its furious energies.

Let me find a task that needs doing. Let me clean a closet, attack the basement, the attic—their clutter too is an enemy.

Let me pour out my anger upon them, throwing out things that get in the path of my existence. Let me clean house, literally as well as emotionally.

I can cry a little as I work. That will help get rid of some of the emotion at the same time I'm getting rid of *things*.

Oh, God, your world sometimes seems such a mess.

Your people seem such a mess. My life seems such a mess.

Maybe that's why sometimes we're given these violent fires of anger, sheer anger, to burn a little of the mess away and make our own path clear.

If so, thank you. Bless my anger. And put my anger to some good use.

Self-Pity

Lord, all night I lay awake consorting with self-pity.

Its idiot voice would not let me sleep. It entertained me with its chant of woes.

It pursued me into the pillow when I tried to bury my head. When I turned to the right it was there, insidiously smiling; when I turned to the left it perched upon my bed.

I thrust it aside but it would not leave me; it would not let me go. And though I finally slept, when I awoke this morning, it trailed me into the kitchen triumphant.

It was not satisfied that it had robbed me of rest; it wanted to sit beside me at breakfast, to tag me about all day. It pursues, it clutches at me still.

God, I am asking you to purge me of this awful companion now. I offer it up to you to do with what you will.

Take self-pity away. Banish it. Heal me of its scars.

Please put self-respect, and a vital glowing sense of the many marvels and blessings of my life in its place.

Give Me Patience

Oh, God, give me patience!
With this child who's telling his eager, long-winded story. Let me keep smiling and pretending I'm enthralled. If I don't, if I cut him off he'll not only be hurt, he may not come to me with something really important next time. But, dear Lord, help me to guide him gently to the climax soon.

Oh, God, give me patience!
With this baby who's dawdling over his food. He must eat, the doctor says, and I mustn't coax, threaten, or grab him and shake him as I'm tempted to—even though I know it would only make things worse and damage us both. Help me to sit quietly waiting, waiting, learning patience.

Oh, God, give me patience!
With this boring old lady who wants me to look at all the pictures of her grandchildren and

listen (again) to her oft-told tales. Help me to remember that I may be just as difficult some day, and that by showing warm interest I can add a little joy to her few remaining days. Let me love her instead of resent the time she's taking. Let me gain something from enduring this hour with her. Let me learn through her the lesson of patience.

Oh, God, give me patience—as I wait for a friend who is late, or for a line that's busy, or for traffic to clear. Let me be fully aware of my surroundings as I wait—the feel of the chair upon which I sit, the passing parade of people, or the scent and color and sound of the very air. Help me to realize that no time is really wasted in this life so long as we are fully awake to the moment, so long as we are aware.

Oh, God, give me patience—with myself!

With my follies, my hasty words, my own mistakes. The times when I seem a hopeless bumbler unworthy of friend or family or the company of any human being, so that I get into a panic and think, "Why am I taking up space on the earth? Why can't I flee, vanish into eternity, simply disappear?

Help me to stop wrestling with remorse. Taking a futile inventory. Waking up in the night to berate myself for "things I ought to have done and things I ought not to have done." Reassure me, oh God, that there *is* health and hope and goodness in me, and that if I just have patience they will take over. I'll become the person I want to be and that you expect me to.

On Recovering from an Operation

Well, God, here I am. Coasting back to consciousness.

No longer lost in the black deathlike oblivion, but blessedly reborn. Thank you for reclaiming me.

Thank you for the doctors whose skilled hands worked upon me while I slept.

Thank you for the kind, efficient hands that tend me now.

Thank you for the cool water upon my tongue. For the smooth bed I'm lying on. Thank you even for the pain which makes me realize that I am alive. I exist!

Help me to bear that pain with courage. Thank you for the knowledge that "This too shall pass."

For now, Lord, give me strength. Let your love sustain and comfort me. Let it flow through me to bless and strengthen everyone in this hospital, and all who are concerned for me.

Let the purifying force of this experience make me a finer person. More understanding of other people's suffering. More appreciative of a whole and healthy body.

More aware of the joy of living in this beautiful world to which, thank God, you have let me come back.

Making a Speech

Dear Lord, please help me make this speech. Please stop my knees from shaking, and quiet the heart in my breast. Instead of fear, fill me with joy at this opportunity to share my thoughts with others.

Please let those thoughts be worth hearing, and give me the words to express them well. But don't let me take myself too seriously, or worry if I make a mistake.

Help me to remember that to be warm and human is generally to be interesting; that to be honest is generally to be effective; and that a laugh is worth more than empty eloquence.

Let me avoid generalities and high-sounding abstractions; let me speak in parables, the way you did.

Give me some small human measure of your divine yet simple power. Oh, Christ, who moved the multitudes, help me to reach this one small crowd.

Thank you for being with me as I make this speech.

My Body

been made to serve so amply, so well, so long. And until the day comes when I'll have no . . . . . of . . . . to the

Thank you, God, for this body.

For the things it can feel, the things it can sense, the wondrous things it can do.

For its bright vigor at the day's beginning, for the hard sweet satisfaction of it walking, working, playing. For its very weariness at the day's end, and the dear comfort of it sleeping. Sometimes for even its pain—if only to sting me into some new awareness of my own existence upon this earth.

I look upon it sometimes in reverent amazement—for we are indeed fearfully and wonderfully made. All its secret silent machinery meshing and churning, all its muscles coordinating, the whole of it so neatly functioning.

Lord, don't let me hurt it, scar and spoil it, overindulge it or overdrive it, but don't let me coddle it either. Let me love my body enough to keep it agile and able and well, strong and clean.

Thank you that I live within this body—the real, eternal, forever existing me. That it has been made to serve me so happily, so well, so long. And until the day comes when I'll have no further need of it, let me appreciate it to the fullest and be grateful for it: my body.

The Compliment

I want to suggest a new Beatitude: "Blessed are the sincere who pay compliments."

For I have just had a compliment, and it has changed my day.

I was irritated. Tired. Discouraged. Nothing seemed much use. Now suddenly all this is changed.

I feel a spurt of enthusiasm, of energy and joy. I am filled with hope. I like the whole world better, and myself, and even you.

Lord, bless the person who did this for me.

He probably hasn't the faintest idea how his few words affected me. But wherever he is, whatever he's doing, bless him. Let him too feel this sense of fulfillment, this recharge of fire and faith and joy.

Thank you, God, for this simple miracle so available to all of us. And that we don't have to be saints to employ its power.

Remind me to use it more often to heal and lift and fortify other lives: a compliment!

A Blessing in Time of Defeat

Lord, someone else has won the honor that I thought should be mine. Bless him.

Someone else is enjoying the rewards I expected. Bless him.

Help me to remember that there is enough fame to go around. Enough money to go around. Enough happiness.

And if I have not found mine this time, there will be other opportunities.

This time maybe I wasn't ready. Next time I will be. Or the next time after that.

Purge me of resentment; heal me of malice; soothe my disappointment. Don't let me impede my own progress by such emotions.

Instead, let me ask a blessing upon the one who has beaten me. To do so is to strengthen myself. To do so is to draw upon a new source of energy and courage and optimism.

I will rise up from defeat with joy. I will go forward enriched by this experience, spiritually growing.

And as I bless I will be blessed. Thank you for this knowledge.

God, help me to stop making comparisons.

Let me remember that each life must follow its own course, and that what happens to other people has absolutely nothing to do with what happens to me.

Help me to stop trying to judge—either others, society, or you. Help me to judge only my own performance in the light of the talent, health, and opportunities you have given me.

When I fail help me to stop blaming other people for my failures, God—or blaming you.

But help me not to blame myself too much either.

Help me to keep faith in myself, as well as faith in your will for me.

Forgive Us Our Excesses

Oh, Lord, these excesses! These sad excesses. So destructive of body and spirit, and bringing such sorrow into the circles of love. . . .

Help us all to remember that excess in anything *is* a sickness of the spirit. Whether it be eating too much or drinking too much or taking too many pills. (Or wanting love too much—wandering, seeking the not-to-be-found assurance in infidelity.)

Surely in going to these excesses we are sor-

rowing for ourselves, because *life itself* seems
too much.

We reach for these crutches to enable us to
sustain it. Or to comfort ourselves, to escape or
to minimize its pain. Self-indulgence is surely
only a form of self-pity and self-scorn.

Oh, God, forgive us these mortal weaknesses,
and help us to forgive them in each other. Help
us to understand that they spring from suffering
at the core of the very soul.

Share with us your wisdom so that we'll know
how to help each other, sustain each other, comfort each other, provide such loving awareness
of each other that we won't need the false assurance of these excesses.

Thank you for delivering us from self-
indulgence and restoring our self-respect.

I Am So Tired

You, who said, "Come unto me all ye who are
weary and heavy-laden and I will give you rest,"
I come to you now.

For I am weary indeed. Mentally and physically I am bone-tired. I am all wound up, locked
up tight with tension. I am too tired to eat. Too
tired to think. Too tired even to sleep. I feel close
to the point of exhaustion.

Lord, let your healing love flow through me.

I can feel it easing my tensions. Thank you. I can feel my body relaxing. Thank you. I can feel my mind begin to go calm and quiet and composed.

Thank you for unwinding me, Lord, for unlocking me. I am no longer tight and frozen with tiredness, but flowing freely, softly, gently into your healing rest.

Violence

This violence, Lord. I am confused by all this violence. Where is Christ in the cruel violence that fills our newspapers, our movie and TV screens, and walks the city streets?

Love your neighbor, he said, but love your enemies too. Give the robber your cloak, turn the other cheek. For God is love, he taught us. That is the whole secret of our relationship to each other and to you. To love, to show compassion, and to live in peace.

Yet this violence, Lord. All this violence. Isn't it enough that there is no respite from the savagery of war? Are we to have no respite from man's inhumanity to man even in our homes? Murder for amusement! My children (if I'd let them) sitting entranced before programs where people knife, gouge, stamp, shoot, hang, strangle each other. Not kindness, not compassion, not even reason—but raw brute viciousness.

How can we find any significance in Christ's suffering if the spectacle of human suffering is so cheap and commonplace?

And the actual violence that lurks beyond our doors.

When a daughter is late coming home from the library, I worry. My faith and fears are at war. It isn't safe for any woman to walk alone, even by daylight any more.

Your stars are so bright tonight, and the air is sweet with spring. I want to take the dog for a run, but a boy walking his dog was assaulted by a gang last week and beaten so badly he may not live. . . . Even a dog may not be protection; even a church. A friend, driving home from a prayer service, was kidnapped by a man hidden in the back seat. And her screams for help went unheeded by people passing by.

We're afraid even to be good Samaritans any more.

Yet how can Christians live in fear? How can we love and help each other if we live in fear?

What would Christ have done about all this violence?

I know he would never have huddled behind locked doors. He would have walked forth bravely, still teaching his truths of peace, of love. But just as he drove the money changers from the temple, he would have lashed out too against those who would destroy the soul as well as the body through violence.

God, let me and my family live in a world of violence unafraid. But give us the mental and moral strength to combat this violence the way Christ would.

Kindness

> Inasmuch as ye have done it unto one of the least of these, my brethren, ye have done it unto me.

MATTHEW 25:40

Lord, my faults are many. And the faults of my children are many. But whatever our sins and failings, help us never to be guilty of any conscious cruelty. Keep us always kind.

The world is so full of suffering. Unspeakable suffering on the grand scale; desperate lonely suffering in the small events of human life: Failures, disappointments, secret agonies.

Help us never knowingly to contribute to that suffering, either by a physical act or a gloating word. Don't let us ever rejoice in another's pain or downfall; let us share that pain as Christ would have done, and help each other instead.

Kindness, oh Lord. Simple human kindness.

We are all so hungry for it—to give it and to receive it—yet we are so afraid. Afraid to reach out and touch each other lest we be rejected. Or afraid of being conspicuous. And so we hold back the kindness that often begs to be released. We lock our lips against the healing words, we look the other way.

Or we hug our privacy tightly about us for protection, and its shell grows hard. Often, on guard against hurt, we stab out at each other, like animals whose instinct is to strike first in order to survive. But we are not animals who must destroy each other; we are your children. And Christ was your living symbol sent to teach us compassion and love.

Through kindness, simple human kindness, we are uplifted. We stand for a shining moment in your presence; we know for an instant the very source of goodness from which we came.

God keep us from cruelty always. God keep us close to you through kindness.

Just for Today

Oh, God, give me grace for this day.

Not for a lifetime, nor for next week, nor for tomorrow, just for this day.

Direct my thoughts and bless them.

Direct my work and bless it.

Direct the things I say, and give them blessing too.

Direct and bless everything that I think and speak and do. So that for this one day, just this one day, I have the gift of grace that comes from your presence.

Oh, God, for this day, just this one day, let me live generously, kindly, in a state of grace and goodness that denies my many imperfections and makes me more like you.

Bring Back the Children

Hear, O heavens, and give ear, O earth, for the Lord hath spoken, I have nourished and brought up children, and they have rebelled against me.

ISAIAH 1:2

I'm Tired of Being a Parent

"They grow up so fast," we're told. "Parenthood is all too brief." And this is true. I know the day will come when I'll miss all this acutely.

But right now, oh, Lord, I'm tired of being a parent.

I'm tired of Scout meetings and music lessons and Bluebirds and chaperoning dances and mothers' clubs. And oh, God, so tired of P.T.A.

I've heard all the issues and speeches and problems so many times. I'm bored, God, I'm fed up with thinking about children, talking about children. The common denominator of parenthood can get just too common.

Stir me up again, God. Waken me, return a little of the enthusiasm I felt as a young new parent eager to raise the perfect child in a perfect world.

For the sake of these later children fire me afresh, even though the fire is banked by experience and, I hope, some wisdom gained.

Husband and Son

Dear Lord, please bless the coming session between my husband and our son.

Thank you for draining hostility from them, and in its place generating love.

Thank you for making them forget past conflicts. Make them conscious instead of their many hours of companionship, the happy memories they have. I know you will.

Thank you for turning my husband's thoughts back to his own boyhood. Bless him for remembering how he felt at our son's age. This will help him to understand. Thank you for that understanding.

Bless our boy and give him understanding too. Thank you.

Please minimize his rebellion; give him the independence he needs, yes, but also give him respect. Give him some concept of the responsibility it is to be a father, a man.

I claim these things for him in this hour to come.

I claim for both of them patience and reasonableness and love.

I ask and thank you for these things in the name of both God the father, and Jesus the son. Please let these two people who are so dear to me be not divided but, like you, truly one.

A Boy's First Car

Dear Lord, please bless this boy and his first car.

Bless his pride in it, his joy in it, his plans for it.

Let it be whole and sound and right and good for him. Let it carry him safely.

Lord, bless his energies—may they be equal to cope with it (and pay for it).

Bless his mind—may it learn from the mechanical experiences he will have with this car. And may he learn from the emotional experiences this car is going to bring.

Oh, God, give my son judgment in operating this car.

Give him joy without recklessness, power without folly.

Give him generosity and dignity and decency and common sense.

Lord, I offer them up to you for blessing and safe-keeping: This boy. This car.

Going to Church with a Daughter

Thank you for this wonderful way to begin the week.

How nice it is to go to church with a daughter, Lord. What a lovely thing, whether she's two or ten or twenty.

What a blessing, the Sunday morning rites of dressing. Even the inevitable commotion about what to wear. Even the inevitable men's scolding about being late.

Thank you, Lord, for the pleasure of setting off at last and of slipping into a pew feeling— pretty. For a daughter is like wearing a personal adornment, a piece of shining jewelry or a living flower.

People smile upon us. They pay her compliments, which are in essence mine too. For a daughter is a kind of special tribute, an achievement, a joyous adjunct and projection of mother.

Thank you for the privilege of kneeling beside this daughter, reading the responses together, finding the place for her. Or when she's older and I can't find my glasses, having her sure finger find the place for me.

What a blessing, to sing the hymns together. To join voices in the old familiar tunes, or struggle with the new ones. To have eyes meet sometimes, puzzled or in amusement, and remember how my mother and I used to exchange these glances in church together long ago.

Thank you for the special harmony there is between mothers and daughters in church together, Lord, whatever our differences at home. Thank you for this wonderful way to begin the week.

The Tower of Strength

God, is there no respite from the demands of a family?

I don't mean the errands, the physical emergencies, the clothes, even the conferences at school. I mean these emotional demands.

Why must a mother always be the peacemaker? She only gets bloodied and bruised in the process. I want my family to solve their own conflicts, I want them to get along.

But they turn to me for everything. They expect me to be all wise, all sufficient, to have all the remedies, all the answers. The tower of strength is getting tired.

I feel sometimes as if I'm being chopped up and fed to everybody in little pieces. They gobble my time, they drain my energies, they engorge my emotions. I feel riddled, assailed, sucked dry, a living sacrifice to everybody.

Psychiatrists would probably say I enjoy all this or I wouldn't endure it.

Lord, you know better. However I love them, something within wildly protests this destruction. But how can I turn them away without being selfish? Dare I refuse to hear them, or try to help them?

Give me some answers, Lord. For their sake as well as my own, guide me.

Rescue This Child

Oh, God, please help my child. He has no direction, no goal. He's wandered away from so much that he used to be, or that you, his creator, would have him be.

And I am not only worried sick about this, God, I feel guilty. I search my own behavior asking, "Why? Why? What have I done to bring this about? Where have we, his family, failed?" That he, with all his goodness and beauty, his brains, his tremendous potential, should be so lost. Right now it's as if he's nobody going nowhere, at a time when the rest of the world is on its way.

Dear God, please find and restore my wandering child. Arouse in him a sense of purpose, steady him, set him upon his rightful path, and walk with him.

We who love him can't do it. Only you who love him even more can do it.

I offer him to you now, whole and beautiful and filled with promise, the way you sent him to us. Thank you for helping him become the person you meant him to be.

Oh, God, help me to equip my children to resist temptation.

Don't let me expect perfection of them, or demand perfection of myself. But help me to equip my children to live decent happy lives in a world where it is so hard to be good.

We have taken your beautiful world and damaged it so badly for them. We have filled it with physical threat and moral dangers. All this propaganda for sexual license, Lord; for breaking laws we don't like; all the drinking—and now these soul- and mind-scarring drugs.

Oh, dear God, arouse in me such a strong sense of what is truly right and truly wrong that I can convey it to them. Give me the words to express these things, and the courage to say them.

God, keep me close to my children, so that they aren't afraid to talk to me freely. And give me the patience to listen, no matter how inconvenient the times when they come.

Give me understanding, God. Give me wisdom. The wisdom to guide them, and the wisdom to keep still when that is best. Don't let me invade their privacy. Don't let me try to live their lives for them. Don't ever let me betray their trust.

God, fortify me so that I can fortify my children. Give me the strength of character to dem-

onstrate through my own behavior what I claim
to believe.

Oh, God, help me to equip my children to live
decent happy lives in a world where it is so hard
to be good.

For Those We Are Trying to Help

Oh, God, I sometimes get so discouraged trying to pray character into other people.

Over and over I ask: Give them honor. Give
them self-discipline. Give them determination,
give them courage. And when they falter my
disappointment is overpowering. I am bewil-
dered. I am stung.

Why don't you hear me? I wonder. Why don't
you stir the fires within them? Why don't you
rouse them to a sense of their own values? Why
don't you take them in hand and make them the
strong fine people they were meant to be?

Then I realize—you can't do it for them.
I can't do it for them.
They've got to do it for themselves.
And how can I help to give them strength if
I weaken? How can I be a channel of courage if
I become afraid?

Dear Lord, please ease these pangs of parenthood.

The labor of delivering a child is as nothing compared to this anguish. This second, later delivery of the spirit is worse, far worse. It eats the heart, it drinks the blood, it wrenches the very loins.

It could destroy me utterly if I gave way to it. Lord, don't let me. Lord, sustain me. God, give me strength.

God, help me in my grief and disappointment for my child.

Lord, give me comfort.

You who said, "Suffer the little children to come unto me," spare a little tenderness for the mothers and fathers. Suffer us, the parents, to come unto you too.

When a Son Goes to War

His clothes came back today, Lord. The clothes of my boy, who isn't old enough to vote yet, only old enough to kill. I've just unpacked them and put them away, Lord—his crumpled socks, his scuffed loafers, the bright plaid shirt he wore, and the underwear. (I wish I'd gotten the shorts whiter; why didn't he *tell* me they were torn?)

But it's too late for regrets. Whatever I did for him or failed to do has been done. I can't call him back from this the way I could when he was just playing war in the yard—bang, bang, you're dead! I can't yell, "Now you kids stop fighting, you're going to hurt each other." (Though I am yelling silently the same words, somewhere inside: *Men, men, stop fighting, stop hurting each other.*)

I couldn't stop him, Lord, and I don't think even you, who symbolize peace, would have wanted me to. "I don't believe in war or killing, but I won't get out of it either," he said. "This is my country, and if it needs me I'll go and get it over with."

Get it over with. . . . Those words haunt me. I try not to let them, I deny their awful possibility. His life, his young life is only beginning . . . and will it ever be over with? Will wars ever truly be over with and stop?

What a strange world—forgive me, God—you've given us. Animals eating each other. *Men* eating each other. The butchery, the carnage. Are men no better than beasts? We, who were made in your image? We, whom your own son came to teach the patterns of peace?

"Peace, where is your peace?" the women implore. But war is too big for women, or women's prayers. Perhaps we too are only beasts of burden. The burden of the children we carry in our bellies, and carry always in our hearts, wherever they are. And the weight is insupportable, it brings us literally to our knees in a time of war.

This is the burden of women since the world

began. Women have no enemies but war. It is only the men who make war.

Yet war itself is man's enemy too. My son's dearest enemy as he gives up his girl and his school and his car and sends back a little bundle of clothes to be put away, like his life, in a dresser drawer. Our men, our good, decent, fair-minded men, are weary of bearing the world on their shoulders, sick of the bloody finger which keeps beckoning, "This too is your job, this too is your war."

Yet they go. Because they *are* decent and fair. Hating it, yet they go, as my son has gone. Because there will be no rest for the men or peace for the women so long as any nation, denying you, enslaves its own people; and through walls and barbed-wire fences and armed watchtowers tries to force that way of enslavement and God-denial upon other people everywhere.

And so, Lord, it's with pride as well as pain that I put these clothes away. The crumpled socks, the gaudy shirt, the underwear. Thank you for my son, for his willingness to do his part.

A Blessing for Family Trials

Bless every circumstance of this, my life.
Bless the bad of it as well as the good of it. For out of the bad of it will surely come further good.

Out of its problems I will arise stronger. Out of its sorrows I will emerge wiser and purer and better equipped to cope with what is yet to come.

Even my family will benefit from these troubles and trials, for in them they too are being tested.

They will emerge better, stronger people. They will become more mature. For their life stories are being written in blood and fire as well as love.

God, help us all to see these truths.

Bless us in our hours of family affliction. Though they may be hours that separate us now, bless them . . . bless them.

For out of our conflicts will come understanding, and out of understanding stronger union, and deeper people, and more lasting, significant love.

The Ledgers of Love

Oh, Lord, let me not dwell on the ingratitude of sons and daughters. . . . Bless them.

Let me not call up a list of their faults and failings. . . . Help them.

Deliver me from the miserable mental balance sheets that my weak foolish nature keeps trying to make come out right.

Help me to remember that whatever most of us do for our children we do out of instinct, duty, and our own pleasure in doing it. . . . Thank you for those things, which were their own reward.

God, bless my own parents who did so much for me, and whom I probably failed and hurt unknowingly many times. Let their kindness, common sense, and forgiveness fill me now and flow out to my sons and daughters, who cannot realize.

When they're too busy to write or call, when they seem to me thoughtless, inconsiderate, even cruel—forgive them, bless them, and ease the strain of their lives.

Give me the gift of understanding, God. You, who must understand and forgive so much of all of us, your children, please guide me now.

Let me judge not, that I be not judged.

The accounts are closed. The ledgers of love are balanced. Thank you for this freeing knowledge, Lord.

So Proud

Oh, Lord, sometimes my delight and pride in my children are almost too much to be contained.

I would praise you for them, I would rejoice—almost I would run dancing into the street.

These sons, so tall and strong. Often as I despair of them, complain of them, their achievements thrill me, their values never cease to surprise me. Their fervor for the underdog, their basic decency, their compassion.

And their unexpected consideration. Just when I think they have failed me they will do something so generous, so thoughtful, I am astonished.

Thank you, God, for these difficult, curious, incredible sons!

And these daughters. So pretty, so poised, so full of life and sweetness.

Not always—no, not always—but growing in grace and charm and womanly loveliness.

They too are a marvel. Where did they come from, these radiant strangers? How is it that my body shaped them, this turbulent household produced them? Yet there they are, demanding so much, yet giving so much in return.

I am ashamed of the way I worry and fret and scold about them. They are so good, so basically kind and good.

Thank you, God, for these daughters.

And my children's accomplishments. Hear, oh Lord, and be patient with me in my pride.

They don't always excel, but when they do my gratefulness and pride are almost too much.

The honor roll (at last!). The team. The chorus. (That's my child, I want to tell everyone, the best looking one in the second row.) The plays. The recitals. I sit on my hands to restrain my applause. I lock my lips against bragging. Yet my eyes and my heart are urging the whole world to take notice.

No, no, I dare not proclaim this pride in them to others. But you who fashioned them and sent them to me, you to whom I often cry out my distress, surely you want to hear and share it.

I am proud of these children, Lord. I rejoice in my sons and daughters. Thank you for them!

Bring Back the Children

Lord, it seems sometimes that my arms aren't long enough or my lap isn't big enough. I wish I could stretch my arms out and out to embrace all my children. These, here about the table now, and those who are away, off to their meetings or their dates or far away in their own homes.

I am suddenly aware of them, all of them wherever they are, and the excitement and wonder and pain of their lives are almost too much to comprehend.

I am so thrilled about them, so proud of them, and so worried about them too—all at once. I want suddenly to reach out and touch them, the warmth of their flesh, the feel of their hair, to draw them physically in.

I want to hold them on my lap again, the big

ones and the little ones, all at once. I want to tuck them in their beds under the same familiar roof. I want to lock the door and go to sleep knowing they're all safe in the shelter of this house.

Lord, I wish I could have all my children back —now, this moment, at once. But since I can't, you who are everywhere, reach them for me, keep them safe in the shelter of my love.

The Mavericks

In the Lord put I my trust; how say ye then to my soul, that she should flee as a bird unto the hill?

PSALM 11:1

New to the Kingdom

Lord, I sometimes feel so new to the kingdom. I feel like a gauche, uncertain stranger in a room full of people where everybody else knows each other. And they know you so much better too; most of them, it seems.

They are so at ease, so at home. While I feel insecure, I feel afraid. How is it that I have been invited here along with them? What am I doing here? I ask. Am I really wanted?

All my faults assail me. I think of the times I have forgotten you, denied you, even betrayed you. And I marvel that your doors are still open to me, your table richly spread for me as well.

I am filled with humility and distress. I feel unworthy. As if I must leave before you notice me.

But something deep within me tells me that you are already aware of my having come. And if I left now you would be deeply hurt.

So I cannot escape you, Lord. I have accepted your invitation. I have come.

Thank you for helping me to feel worthy of you, Lord. Thank you for letting me feel truly wanted.

To Build Up Faith

God, please help me to build up my faith.

Let me understand that faith is not a blind acceptance, but a certain and reasonable knowledge.

Not a gift bestowed upon favored people, but a powerful conviction achieved through serious effort.

God, guide me to people who can encourage me in my faith. (Thank you for such people.)

Lead me to books that will enlighten and enhance my faith. (Thank you for such books.)

Show me works both human and divine that prove that you do exist and love us. Open my eyes to your many wonders.

Free my cluttered and limited mind from its confusions. Release it, refresh it, widen it so that into it may flow an appreciation of your vast, shining, limitless intelligence. (Thank you for that clearing and that comprehension now.)

Help me to practice my faith, for only through practice can it grow in me. Oh, God, remind me to reach you and understand you, and renew my faith through prayer.

But It Doesn't Fit My Plans

Lord, let me not be so impatient when my life doesn't go according to my plans.

Let me remember that there are many ways to serve you, many paths by which to reach you.

Help me not to be so baffled when I start one direction and seem to find you leading me another.

I am often dismayed. I protest. I waste valuable time insisting, "No, no, I can't, I won't!"

Then your hand steadies me. I go forward—not always willingly, but at least without resistance—and lo, the course is often more fulfilling than that which I had chosen for myself.

Lord, help me to remember this when I am shocked and disheartened at the changing of my plans.

Let me trust in your wisdom.

Let me flow cheerfully into the stream of your will.

The New Concept

Christ, I have a new concept of you.

Suddenly I see you real—not mystical but human—sitting across from me almost as a doctor would. Instead of a doctor's face I see yours, the face of the great physician. And with this comes a marvelous, almost shocking realization: You can heal me if I will let you.

I see you too as a wise counselor. I think of the people in authority to whom I have turned—a psychologist, a teacher, a judge. Suddenly I am staggered to realize that you are all these people in one.

I don't have to make an appointment, I can turn to you any time I need. You will listen, you will guide me about my husband, my child, my job, my very human concerns.

For you were human too. You are human still. For you live and walk the earth with me and with all these others whom you have made. You understand these awful conflicts.

And so now, right now, I lay this latest problem before you. What can I do? You know how desperately I've tried—where have I erred? How can I change this situation?

Even if I cannot hear your counsel, I can feel it. Your strength and your wisdom flow into me. From you I draw the ability to change what I can, but endure what I must.

The Suffering

Right now, Lord, my faith in you is shaky. The light that sometimes floods me with your presence is dim.

Today I saw sorrow, suffering, deprivation. And I am haunted by these things. I cannot root them out of my mind and concentrate on your love.

Why? I keep asking. Why is it that you can be so good to me, and let these, your children, remain in want?

I saw a little girl who couldn't go to school because she didn't have a pair of shoes. I saw an ugly old woman dying of cancer in a hovel overrun by rats. I saw a boy who has lost his eyesight and both legs in war.

Where are you, God, as I unlock my door and enter my quiet house? How can you be here with me, waiting like a gentle lover, to listen and to encourage and comfort me?

Are you in the heart of the old woman? Are you telling the boy who'll never see his sweetheart to buck up, things are going to be all right? What are you saying to the little girl who is crying because she can't go to school? How can she understand?

God, my heart and soul are sick.

All I can say is help them, help them. Draw as near to them as you seem, at times, to be to me. Bless their existence, bless their wants, bless their minds and bodies, bless their suffering to some purpose that right now I simply cannot see.

I Ask for Things That Do Not Come

Oh, God, my faith is often on such shaky ground.

I wish it were not so, but it is true.

I ask for things that do not come. I urge you for things that do not happen.

"Ask and you shall receive," the Scriptures say. "Knock and the door will be opened." Yet the door remains fast. Though my knuckles are bloody from knocking, and my voice is hoarse from asking. This is so hard to accept when we don't know why. We cannot understand.

Sometimes I don't even *ask* for things, so blind is my faith that they will come. (Isn't this prayer too?) And so convinced am I that the cause is right and just. Then when all is denied me I am astounded, I feel betrayed. I begin to pray, pray hard, but no longer in the blind innocence of faith.

Doubts fill me. Fears invade.

Sometimes I don't trust you, God. But this is worse than not trusting someone you love.

It is self-divisive; very lonely.

I need your presence, and behind that presence a sense of the validity of your promises.

God, help me not to make my faith dependent upon the things I pray for and don't get.

You Don't Have to Choose Up Sides

God, it does not help my faith to be with blind and credulous people who have inherited their religion. Or whose beliefs are package-mixed and who accept you only because they have never questioned you, because they do not think.

In many ways they are worse than the skeptics, the agnostics and atheists who doubt you or deny you altogether.

I cannot abide dumb or bigotted people. I want to flee to the intellectuals. I want to be on the side of people who at least have some logical reasons for what they think.

Lord, help me to remember that I don't have

to choose up sides. That my own faith has nothing to do with either kind of people.

Faith is my own private need of you reaching out to find you.

Faith is my own intelligence responding to yours.

My faith is my knowledge that in your vast intelligence you created this world—and me.

My faith is my growing conviction that you are not off somewhere running the universe, but here, now, with me. That you care about me.

Thank you for this faith.

The Mavericks

Lord, some people seem to graze like sheep in the placid pastures of their faith.

Some of them were born there and never broke away from your fold. Others, after some wandering, found shelter there and are quiet and content. They look with a bland mystification upon the mavericks.

They don't quarrel and question and rebel. They don't fight with you, God; they don't despair.

They follow you, their shepherd, with a blind abiding trust. They eat the sweet grasses beneath their feet, they drink the cool waters, and at night they lie down safely in the fold.

Did you choose them, Lord? In fashioning their natures did you separate these placid and trusting ones from the goats?

I envy them their gentle spirits, Lord. I envy them the peaceful paths they follow across the meadows of their faith.

I don't want to stray. I don't want dogs and devils nipping at my heels.

Yet I wonder sometimes if you didn't deliberately make some of us so—if only to keep things from being too easy for yourself.

Is it just possible that you like to have a few mavericks that have to be chased and herded back?

Bring Us Together

The Lord be between thee and me forever.

FIRST SAMUEL 20:23

For a Friend

I don't believe I've ever thought to thank you, God, for this wonderful friend. But I do thank you for creating her and letting her enrich my life this way.

Thank you for all the years we've known each other and the confidences and hopes and troubles that we've shared.

Thank you for the understanding we bring to each other. For the patience we have with each other's faults; for the advice and even the scoldings we are able to give each other without either of us taking offense.

Thank you for the help we have been to each other—in this way, and so many more. Thank you that because of her I am a better, happier person, and that she has grown as a person too because of me.

Thank you that she would give me anything in her power—time, money, work, possessions, encouragement, sympathy— whatever my need. And that she knows I would be as quick to respond to whatever her needs might be.

Thank you that we can laugh together, cry together, rejoice together. And although we may not see each other for a long time, when we do come together it is always the same.

Lord, bless and keep her, this person you fashioned and filled with qualities that have meant so much to me. Lord, thank you for my friend.

Oh, Lord, my two best friends are lunching together today and I'm worried sick. Please don't let them tell each other the foolish things that, in unguarded moments, I have said about each of them. I am filled with remorse. I ask your forgiveness for those things.

You know that I love each of them dearly.

You know that I would never intentionally hurt either of them.

You know how much I value their friendship. And I know that they value mine.

Humbly I lay this situation before you for blessing: Three women who are very close to each other, but who sometimes criticize each other. Knowing women, I know that they probably criticize me too.

If they do so today, I know they don't mean it unkindly. But don't let me find out. Spare me foolish tongues.

If they discuss me, above all don't let either of them repeat anything I've said. Spare them my foolish tongue.

Bless them both. Bless their time together. Don't let anything threaten it. Bless their friendship—and mine.

And in the future, help me. Guard, oh guard, I pray, my foolish tongue.

Teach Us How to Speak

I'm tired of all this empty talk, Lord. The shrill exchanges at parties, the dull discussions at meetings, the meaningless banalities of greetings on the street. All our dreary accounts of our ailments or our children or the price of eggs.

You, who gave us the marvelous gift of language, must despair. Why do we go through life with our mouths open letting these inanities pour out as an excuse for speech?

There is beauty within each of us, Lord, for you made us perfect, in your image, and you are there.

There is nobility and goodness surely, through your indwelling presence.

But we are so dumb and lonely and anxious and inept when we try to communicate. In our poor efforts to reach each other we hold back, our lips are locked lest we reveal what we truly think and feel. It is as if we are afraid to acknowledge the living God within us, perfect and whole. Our outward imperfections stop us, our petty concerns. We are ashamed to lay claim on beauty and significance.

Oh, God, please help us to speak freely to each other, with more dignity, joy, and purpose. Deliver us, Lord, from these empty locks of talk.

Who Are My Neighbors?

Who are my neighbors, Lord? Who are truly my neighbors?

They exist in their great houses, set so far apart on the commanding hills, and if they need or want me or we might enjoy each other, I don't know it. And I am afraid to go seeking them out lest I intrude.

Who are my neighbors, Lord? Who are truly my neighbors?

Others cluster close, too close for comfort, up and down the street. I watch their antlike coming and going, puzzled and unsure. They are so frantically busy about nothing, or so it seems. They talk, talk, talk about nothing.

I am afraid of getting too close to them, for I don't want to be gobbled up in the empty talk and the empty activity.

Yet I am hungry for neighbors, Lord, true neighbors on whom I can depend and who can depend on me. I long for their occasional companionship, for their understanding, for the knowledge that they are there, willing and wanting to share joy and sorrow with me.

Dear Lord, help me to know who are truly my neighbors, and bring us together so that we can help each other in the timeless ways that neighbors always have.

The Older People

Lord, help me to remember to be nicer to older people. Let me take time for them.

Remind me that we are all on the selfsame journey, and each day takes us nearer to the time when we too may be standing on the sidelines of life waiting for someone to speak to us, take an interest in us, draw us back in.

Make me more thoughtful of older people, Lord. Let me be a comfort to them, a help to them, a joy to them. And let this be not a duty but a conscious seeking of values that will restore a sense of value to them.

Let me learn from their wisdom, be enriched by their experience. Let me glimpse, through their eyes, a vision of the thrilling length, yet the startling brevity of life, and its tremendous significance.

Thank you, God, for the older people, who are a tangible testimony to these things. Let me take time for them.

The Unexpected

Thank you, Lord, for these unexpected moments of love.

For the times in life when suddenly we feel your nearness uniting us with other people.

I felt it so keenly yesterday. In a small group of people—not family, not even close friends. Actually, I had never felt any real attachment for any of them, and some I thought rather dull.

But suddenly, sitting around the fire, they became dear—very dear. Qualities I hadn't noticed before became manifest. Kindness, tenderness, gaiety, goodness.

You were suddenly with us, uniting us, your children. Revealing us to each other in a new dimension. Giving us understanding.

I felt my antagonism toward one of them melting, giving way to joy. A new awareness of another came to me; I saw a charm, a loveliness unsensed before.

And as my new-sensed love flowed out to them I felt their love encompassing me. We were brothers and sisters all, needing and wanting each other.

We were your children together around the hearthfire of life. We were your family.

When Someone Lets You Down

Someone whom I love and trust has betrayed me.

Someone I believed in has not lived up to that belief. Bless and help him now.

This experience has altered my concept of that person, yes, but don't let it destroy my faith in him altogether. Let me remember, and bless, the rest of the good in him.

Above all, don't let it destroy my faith in other people. For surely faith in our friends, our family, those we work with is one of the dearest things you have given us.

Without it we ourselves are empty and meaningless.

Bless all the people I know and love and deal with. Let us all keep faith with each other as best we can.

Please especially bless the person who has disappointed me, for he needs your help even more. His weakness cries out for your strength.

Bless him, help him. Intensify the good in him.

The Package of Problems

Oh, Lord, I have so many problems I hardly know where to start praying.

Each of them seems important. Many of them seem urgent.

But if I even begin praying about them one by one it will take all morning, and I've so much work to do.

I must also get busy and *work* for many of the people whose problems I need to pray about.

So will you please forgive me and hear me if I package them all up at once and offer them to you?

Please take this large, heavy, complex package and let your love shine through it. Thank you.

Let your healing, cleansing love lighten the package. May it flood through these many problems on through the lives of all these people, blessing them.

Thank you for helping them strip from their lives the things that are causing these problems. Thank you for giving them the wisdom to resolve their difficulties. Thank you for giving them the strength.

Even with your help I don't have enough wisdom for them all. Enough strength. Enough time!

Right now not even the time to pray for them individually.

So thank you for understanding. Thank you for blessing them.

Bring Us Together

Oh, God, we go through life so lonely, needing what other people can give us, yet ashamed to show that need.

And other people go through life so lonely, hungering for what it would be such a joy for us to give.

Dear God, please bring us together, the people who need each other, who can help each other, and would so enjoy each other.

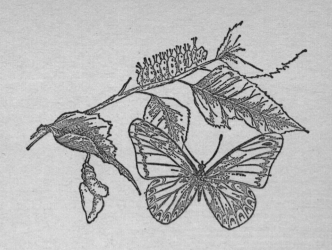

The New Dimension

And I give unto them eternal life, and they shall
never perish.

JOHN 10:28

Oh, God, my God, you have taken my mother away and I am numb with shock.

I see her apron still hanging behind the kitchen door. I see her dresses still in the closet, and her dear shoes there upon the floor.

Her house is filled with her presence. The things she so recently used and touched and loved. The pans in the cupboard. The refrigerator still humming and recent with her food. The flowers she had cut still bright in their bowl upon the table.

How quickly you called her, how mercifully. She simply stopped what she was doing and looked up—and you were there.

She was ready. She was always completely ready. Yet she must have known that she was going soon. There were bookmarks in her Bible at these passages:

"Though I speak with the tongues of men and of angels and have not charity. . . ." Surely this was her message to us—to be at peace between ourselves. And:

"When Jesus knew that his hour was come that he should depart out of this world unto the Father, having loved his own, which were in the world, he loved them unto the end."

To the end. She loved us too to the very end.

Help us, who were her children, to draw near to each other now. And near to her. And through her, nearer to you.

Thank you, God, for the wonderful lesson of loss.

The arms of my friends console me, the love of my family surrounds me. The goodness and kindness of my neighbors sustain me like a staff.

Though I am prostrate with grief I am supported, as by a great shining column that rises up within me. I can lift up my head, I can walk upright. I can even smile.

For their sympathy is also like a lovely pool in which I see glimpses of goodness and beauty never revealed before. In it my agony is soothed, the ache of my heart becomes bearable and will, I know, one day heal.

Surely if human beings can surround and help and support each other in such times of sorrow, then your love, oh God, must be even more great.

I feel your kind hand upon me through the touch of theirs. I feel your promises fulfilled.

I see my dear one fresh and new and whole, free of pain and problems, spared of all distress. I see that dear one lifted up into some new state so joyful and free and ongoing that excitement fills me.

I sense that blessed presence saying, "It is true! It really is. Believe this, oh believe this and don't grieve."

I am enriched by this loss. My faith is renewed. I am a better person for it.

God of our creation, God of our ongoing, thank you for this wonderful lesson of loss.

Be Still and Know

Oh, God, death is so still, so utterly still.

Death is more still than the quietest meadow on a summer day. Stiller than the whitest snows of a winter hillside. More deeply still than the deepest stillness of a starry night.

There is such peace in death, for the spirit is lost in the bliss of some absolute dream.

Death is perfect acceptance, perfect understanding.

Death is the perfect knowing.

"Be still and know that I am God," you said. The living can never attain that absolute perfection of stillness and knowing. Only the dead.

But so profound is their stillness this we do know: In you they live.

The New Dimension of Love

I know that they live again, that they live again, my dear ones whom I no longer can see.

You have not taken them into a kingdom—they wouldn't be happy in a kingdom—but you have opened wide for them a place of joy and peace and challenge, where their dreams can be fulfilled.

And this place somehow includes my own small portion of the world. They have not really left me, my dear ones, they are close by me in a way they could never be before.

They know how much I miss them, they know how much I love them. They understand about all the things I meant to do for them and didn't, the words I failed to say.

They put their arms around me to comfort me. They tell me, "It's all right, human love is faulty but for all its faults enduring. It goes beyond such things, it goes beyond even this separation. The loss of the body does not mean the loss of that love. There is a new life in which that love is even stronger. For God is love, remember. God is truly love."

And this I know. This, God, I know: They are with you now—forever. And so with me forever —in this new dimension of love.

When the Winds Cry I Hear You

Thou shalt show me the path of life; in thy presence is the fullness of joy, and at thy right hand there is pleasure for evermore.

PSALM 16:11

Companion

The Lord is my friend and my companion.

How can I ever be lonely so long as he is with me?

He walks along a country road with me and opens my senses to loveliness never noticed before: The glitter of gravel beneath my feet, a tangle of sun-sweet grasses, a dust-colored toad —all are remarkable and fresh.

He accompanies me along the busy streets. The shop-windows are newly enticing. The lights dance more brightly upon the pavements. I realize the fragrance of a hot-dog stand, the evening paper, the spicy tang of carnations from a vendor's cart.

The crowds don't overwhelm me. I can look into their passing faces and briefly, joyously know them—for the Lord is within them too.

I can go to a party where all are strangers, yet I am happy and at ease, for my Lord is also there.

I can come home to an empty place, a silent place, yet the Lord enters the room with me and fills it.

I will not hide within the Lord, for I am in the world and of it and his warm living people are dear.

Yet other friends, other companions he will send me in abundance so long as I keep him near.

And whenever others fail me or my spirit needs escape I can turn to the Lord and be at peace.

Through the Voices

How lovely is the sense of communion I feel sometimes, oh God. How sweet is the sense of your nearness.

Sometimes you are so far away. I lose track of you altogether. The noises of living drown you out.

All the voices, the incessant voices: voices on the telephone, voices speaking and singing and crying out from television and radios.

And the voices of my family, the neighbors, people at the office, people on the street. Human voices, pouring out billions of those oral noises we call words. My own voice joining them, pouring out more, but so few of us actually listening, almost none of us capable of understanding.

I want to stop them all sometimes, including my own. I long to cover my ears and run from them, seeking silence, seeking peace.

But then sometimes, in the midst of all the voices, the silence comes unbidden. The sense of your presence, your blessedly voiceless presence, speaking to me without words. And I am soothed. I no longer resist the other voices. They begin to make a kind of music. I have no need to run away.

You are so near, you create the quiet within me. You hush and soften all these sounds of living and make them sweet.

Dance of Worship

Lord, for those of us who love dancing, let us dance sometimes in prayer.

The spirit often physically reaches out toward you. The heart is filled with emotions that words can't always express. The mind teems with problems that often block the path to you.

Lord, as I move to this music I offer up all my feelings. My joy in this beautiful world, my awe and gratitude. My hopes and my dreams.

I offer you too in this dance my doubts and disappointments. My anxieties and grievances. I banish them, I break their chains. I cast them into the music and my body frees my spirit to dance before you as well.

Accept this dance as an act of worship, oh God, and draw near.

And now as I dance I would offer up all the people I should be praying for. As I lift my arms in adoration I gather them in for your blessing.

I see them happy. I see them well. This vision is vivid before me. As I dance I rejoice for their health, their happiness, their peace. These things I claim in your name for them.

I dance for the people I love, oh Lord. I dance their cares into your keeping.

But I also dance for myself. For the joy and wonder of my own being. I dance in worship, to reach you.

The Garden

This is my garden, God, this is my garden, my own small precious portion of the earth that you have made.

I will dig and hoe and tend it, I will grub in the soil that is cool and moist and scented with spring.

I will find you in that soil as I crumble its clods or press these small seeds deep into its dark flesh.

What a joyful thing, the feel of your silent soil. It clings to my fingers, it is hard and certain beneath my knees.

It receives my little offerings—these tiny plants, these slips and cuttings, these infinitesimal seedlings, with a kind of blind, uncommenting magnificence. I am a trifle awed before it, I am filled with an amused humility.

How insignificant I am that I should be entrusted with this miracle to come. No, no, the earth will surely reject my anxious efforts, my foolish hopes. Yet I know a happy patience too. Wait—only wait upon the Lord, as the Bible says.

And sure enough. The silent, teeming forces of creation set to work, and soon the miracle has come! Onions and lettuce for the table. Shrubs to be trimmed. The incredible colors and fragrances of flowers.

I think of that first garden where life began.

I think of that final garden where Christ prayed. ("In my father's house are many mansions," he said. I feel sure that among those mansions there are many gardens too.)

How marvelous that man's existence—and woman's—began in a garden. Perhaps that's why we feel so wonderfully alive in a garden. And so close to you.

The Swim

Dear God, I feel your presence in the great blue arch of sky. How vast you are, it reminds me. How endless your time.

I see birds winging across that blueness and feel a new awarenes of the miracle of flight. I hear their voices ringing and chiming in the trees, and it is as if you had sent them to be messengers—earth's small gay angels—to remind us that you are everywhere, and heaven is here too.

I feel the sun hot upon my skin, see it glittering on the water. And I am newly awake to the miracle of that mighty forge which you put into space to warm and feed us and give us life, to govern the very seasons. The sun, so majestic and beautiful, yet touching me so kindly, lying at my feet in a joyous twinkling now.

I plunge into the cold of that other miracle, water. And it too is mighty and mysterious, yet like the sun essential to us, a part of each of us.

I feel its brisk tingling; it drives my blood faster, making me vigorously awake and aware, alive. I feel its cleansing strength. I feel it dissolving my problems, washing them away. I feel it supporting me like strong arms.

I know that so long as I trust it, it will sustain me. Yet I know that it expects me to use my own strength and efforts too.

God, I find you everywhere in this beautiful morning, this bright water. As I swim I give myself to your world and your presence in adoration and delight.

When the Winds Cry I Hear You

Oh, God, my God, when the winds cry I hear you, when the birds call I hear you, when the sea rushes in it is like the rushing of my being toward yours.

You are voice of wind and bird and beat of sea. You are the silent steady pulsing of my blood.

I would know you better, I would taste your essence, I would see your face.

Yet these few small senses of mine cannot do more. You have defined their limits, you have set them within a framework from which we can only see and touch and hear and attempt to know these marvels that you have made.

But this too is the marvel—that you are within each of us as well. As we are drawn toward your greatness we are drawn toward the greatness within ourselves.

We are larger beings, we are greater spirits.

The hunger for you kindles a holy fire that makes us kinder, gentler, surer, stronger—ever seeking, never quite finding, but always keenly aware that you are all about us and within us.

You are here.

ABOUT THE AUTHOR

Marjorie Holmes is the author of the highly successful
I'VE GOT TO TALK TO SOMEBODY, GOD; LORD,
LET ME LOVE, and a host of other books, novels, and
magazine articles. The *New York Times* described her as
"an American phenomenon," and the *Washington Post*
as "the housewives' patron saint." For twenty-five years
her column LOVE AND LAUGHTER was a popular
feature of the *Washington Star*. She also wrote the
column A WOMAN'S CONVERSATION WITH GOD
for *Woman's Day* magazine. She has taught writing
courses at the University of Maryland, Catholic University, and Georgetown—all in the area of Washington,
D.C. She was born in Storm Lake, Iowa, where she
attended Buena Vista College, before graduating from
Iowa's Cornell College. She has traveled widely, visiting
Israel a number of times to do research for her novels.
She is the mother of four grown children. After the
death of her first husband she married Dr. George
Schmieler, a physician from suburban Pittsburgh, where
she now lives.

HEARTWARMING BOOKS
OF
FAITH AND INSPIRATION

Charles Swindoll

☐	26324	DROPPING YOUR GUARD	$3.50
☐	25923	STRENGTHENING YOUR GRIP	$3.50
☐	27524	HAND ME ANOTHER BRICK	$3.95
☐	27334	THREE STEPS FORWARD TWO STEPS BACK	$3.95
☐	26606	YOU AND YOUR CHILD	$3.50

Robert Schuller

☐	26458	THE BE (HAPPY) ATTITUDES	$3.95
☐	25093	POSITIVE PRAYERS FOR POWER-FILLED LIVING	$3.50
☐	25222	REACH OUT FOR NEW LIFE	$3.50
☐	24704	TOUGH-MINDED FAITH FOR TENDER-HEARTED PEOPLE	$3.95
☐	27332	TOUGH TIMES NEVER LAST BUT TOUGH PEOPLE DO!	$4.50

Og Mandino

☐	27742	CHRIST COMMISSION	$3.95
☐	26084	GIFT OF ACABAR	$3.50
☐	27972	THE GREATEST MIRACLE IN THE WORLD	$3.95
☐	27757	THE GREATEST SALESMAN IN THE WORLD	$3.95
☐	26545	THE GREATEST SECRET IN THE WORLD	$3.50
☐	26975	GREATEST SUCCESS IN THE WORLD	$3.50

Bantam Books, Dept. HF3, 414 East Golf Road, Des Plaines, IL 60016

Please send me the books I have checked above. I am enclosing $_____ (please add $2.00 to cover postage and handling). Send check or money order—no cash or C.O.D.s please.

Mr/Ms _____

Address _____

City/State _____ Zip _____

HF3—12/88

Please allow four to six weeks for delivery. This offer expires 6/89. Prices and availability subject to change without notice.

INSPIRING BOOKS
FROM
AMERICA'S
MOST BELOVED
BESTSELLING
AUTHOR

Marjorie Holmes

☐ 25796	HOLD ME UP A LITTLE LONGER, LORD	$3.50
☐ 26428	I'VE GOT TO TALK TO SOMEBODY, GOD	$3.50
☐ 26384	TO HELP YOU THROUGH THE HURTING	$3.50
☐ 25343	TWO FROM GALILEE	$3.50
☐ 26166	THREE FROM GALILEE	$3.50

Look for these books wherever Bantam Books are sold, or use this page to order.

Heartwarming Books of Faith and Inspiration

Special Offer
Buy a Bantam Book
for only 50¢.

Now you can have Bantam's catalog filled with hundreds of titles plus take advantage of our unique and exciting bonus book offer. A special offer which gives you the opportunity to purchase a Bantam book for only 50¢. Here's how!

By ordering any five books at the regular price per order, you can also choose any other single book listed (up to a $5.95 value) for just 50¢. Some restrictions do apply, but for further details why not send for Bantam's catalog of titles today!

Just send us your name and address and we will send you a catalog!